Ojai Valley Vegetarian Cookbook 2nd Edition

recipes for lacto-ovo vegetarian cooking

By Randy Graham

Ojai Valley Vegetarian Cookbook 2nd Edition

recipes for lacto-ovo vegetarian cooking

By Randy Graham

© November 1, 2015
Randolph B. Graham
All Rights Reserved

Second Edition
Ojai, California

Front Cover Photo: Randy Graham
Edits: Brandy Nightingale

*with respect for my
Valley Vegetarian
readers namaste*

Table of Contents

Introduction

Breads
1. Bannock Bread
2. Spoon Bread
3. Irish Soda Bread
4. Mom's Popovers
5. Peruvian Cornbread
6. Jalapeno Cheese Bread
7. Banana Nut Bread
8. Oatcakes
9. Scots Scones
10. Flatbread

Salads
11. Persimmon and Spinach Salad
12. Edamame Salad
13. Chevre Chaud Salad
14. Wheat Berry Salad
15. Spicy Fava Bean Salad
16. Italian Bread Salad
17. Quinoa Salad
18. Raw Beet Salad
19. Fresh Carrot Salad
20. Chicken-less Salad
21. Guinness Potato Salad
22. Arugula Walnut Pesto Salad
23. Caprese Salad
24. Eggplant and Bell Pepper Terrine
25. Gluten-Free Tabouli
26. Two-Tone Coleslaw

Soups
27 Matzo Ball Soup
28 Jalapeno Corn Chowder
29 Baked Potato Soup
30 Mulligatawny Soup
31 Leek and Potato Soup
32 Lentil Soup
33 Robin's Tortilla Soup
34 Cabbage Soup

Fruits and Vegetables
35 Gran's Carrot Casserole
36 Idaho Potatoes
37 Esquites
38 Rosti
39 Boiling Onions and Raisins
40 Plantains with Chipotle Dip
41 Potatoes Au Gratin
42 Fresh Fruit Risotto
43 Japanese Eggplant
44 Root Vegetables Bake
45 Fenugreek Potatoes

Salsas, Spreads, and More
46 Nopale Salsa
47 Salsa Verde
48 Magic Oatmeal
49 Vodka Sauce
50 Pico de Gallo
51 Chow Chow
52 Jalapenos in Escabeche
53 Hachiya Smoothie
54 Middle Eastern Dip
55 Welsh Rarebit
56 Knishes
57 Roasted Red Pepper Sauce

58 Pimiento Cheese Spread
59 Vegetarian Gravy
60 Shallot Vinaigrette
61 Rice Cakes with Habanero Sauce
62 Lo-Cal Potato Salad
63 Ojai Mojo
64 Dog Biscuits
65 Citrusy Kumquat Chutney
66 Simple Lettuce Wraps
67 Guacamole
68 Mushroom and Garlic Tapas
69 Sundried Tomatoes and Eggplant Spread

The Goodness of Fresh Herbs
70 Basil (Pesto)
71 Tarragon (Creamy Dressing)
72 Oregano (Chilaquiles)
73 Thyme (Cream Cheese Spread)
74 Rosemary (Pasta Sauce)
75 Chives (Vegetable Dip)
76 Parsley (Brown Rice)
77 Mint (Iced Tea)
78 Epazote (Black Beans)

Hearty Entrees
79 Valley Vegetarian Burger
80 Nutty Meatloaf
81 Vegetarian Meatballs
82 Lemongrass Tofu
83 California Dreamin' Burger
84 Tofu Frittata
85 Irish Fondue
86 Mexican Hominy Bake
87 Broccoli-Ricotta Cheese Pie
88 Sprouted Burger
89 Ojai Inca Wrap

90   Crust-less Quiche
91   Tofu Osso Buco
92   Tortellini Pasta Pie
93   Chicken-less Pot Pie
94   Tempeh Stir Fry
95   Cheese and Mushroom Crepes
96   Spicy Collard Greens with Basmati Rice
97   Tamale Pie
98   Cheese and Tomato Pie
99   Lasagna Azteca
100 Garbanzo Tahini Bake
101 Potato Frittata
102 Linguini with Roasted Beets
103 Grits with Roasted Poblano Peppers
104 Curried Butternut and Beets
105 Savory Vegetable Tart
106 Eggplant Parmesan
107 Cannellini Bean Casserole
108 Noodle-less Lasagna

Desserts
109 Ojai Orange Pound Cake
110 Amaranth Pudding
111 Cranberry Christmas Cookies
112 Shortbread Cookies
113 Pumpkin Cookies
114 Bread Pudding
115 Rhubarb Crumble
116 Irish Loaf Cake
117 Carrot Cake
118 Spicy Apple Cake
119 Date and Fig Nut Tart
120 Vegan Bundt Cake

New Recipe
121 Egg and Gruyère Strata

How I Became A Vegetarian

The Valley Vegetarian Website

Index of All Recipe Titles (Alpha)

Index of Vegan Recipes (Alpha)

Index of Gluten-Free Recipes (Alpha)

Introduction

This is a collection of the 120 most popular recipes from the first two years of posts to my Valley Vegetarian blog. There's nothing fancy here, just plain good home-style cooking that appeals to everyone without regard to a specific diet. The recipes tend toward comfort food with a taste of Ojai. Real food for real people. Many have been published in the Ojai Valley News under the header Chef Randy.

All recipes are vegetarian, of course, but what omnivore doesn't like a good side dish of Idaho Potatoes, a hearty main dish of Nutty Meatloaf or Vegetarian Meatballs?

Although all of these recipes are healthy, I find the term healthy to be subjective. Instead of focusing on nutrition, I focus on fresh, fun, and tasty recipes leaving the determination of relative health to you. With a little imagination, many of the recipes can be modified to meet your specific needs.

The Baked Potato Soup, for example, calls for whole milk, but it can be made with 1% milk and still be good. Not as tasty as if made with whole milk, but still good and healthy. If you are vegan, substitute olive oil for butter in the Guinness Potato Salad, use vegan egg substitute in the Spicy Apple Cake, and leave the bleu cheese out of the California Dreamin' Burger.

So what is different in this second edition? There is a new cover with a color photo of one of my most requested recipes, Egg and Gruyère Strata. Look for it as bonus recipe number 121.

May you eat well, eat local, eat fresh!

[4 Mom's Popovers]

Breads

1 Bannock Bread

Bannock bread has been a staple food of wilderness explorers, trappers, prospectors, and immigrants for centuries. Today it takes the form of a large oatcake. In the early 1700s, when my family came to America, it was cooked in a skillet and over an open fire. In my mind's eye, I can see my gggg-grandfather making Bannock with lots of flour, a little sugar, drippings of lard, and when available, fruit. This recipe promises to be a wee bit tastier. No lard, of course! If you are pressed for time, make the dough and store it in a Ziploc bag in the refrigerator for up to three days before baking.

Ingredients:
1 cup whole wheat flour
½ cup all-purpose flour
½ cup rolled oats
2 tablespoons sugar
2 teaspoons baking powder
½ teaspoon salt
2 tablespoons butter (melted)
1/3 cup dried apricots (optional)
¾ cup cold water

Directions:
Preheat oven to 400 degrees.

Combine flours, oats, sugar, baking powder, and salt in a large mixing bowl. Add melted butter, apricots (if using), and water. Add more water if needed to make a sticky dough. With floured hands, pat into a greased 8to inch cake pan (a pie tin works well also). Bake for 20 to 25 minutes.

Cut into wedges and serve with butter and jam. If your diet allows for a lot of cholesterol, serve with clotted cream!**2**

2 Spoon Bread

Corn meal has been used in the United States to make corn pone, crackling bread, corn muffins, corn sticks, hoecakes, Johnny cakes and spoon bread. Spoon bread is perhaps the richest, lightest and most delicious use of all. It is believed to have originated as a water and cornmeal based porridge made by Native Americans. The modern version, which includes eggs, butter and cream, is thought to have originated in Virginia sometime in the 1820's.

Spoon bread is made casserole-style and is meant to be served with a spoon. If you haven't guessed by now, that's how it got its name. Some still spell it as all one word. Either way you spell it, spoon bread is an American classic and is a great side dish for any dinner celebration. I like to serve it at Thanksgiving, as it seems to taste especially good in the fall.

Ingredients:
3 tablespoons butter
1 medium yellow onion (chopped)
1 cup white or yellow corn meal
1½ cups corn kernels (if fresh corn is not available frozen corn works well)
1½ teaspoons salt
5 eggs
1½ cups heavy cream

Directions:
Preheat oven to 350 degrees.

Heat 2 tablespoons butter in a medium skillet over medium heat (do not burn). Add onion and cook, stirring occasionally, until softened – about four minutes. Transfer to a medium bowl and set aside.

Bring 2 cups of water to a boil in a small sauce pan. Slowly pour in corn meal while constantly stirring. Reduce heat to medium low and cook until thickened – about 2 to three minutes. Add to onion mixture. Stir in corn kernels, salt and remaining tablespoon of butter. Mix well.

In a separate bowl, whisk together eggs and cream (nonfat half and half works but is not as tasty). Stir into the onion-corn mixture until well incorporated. Pour into a buttered soufflé or casserole dish. Bake until top is golden – about 1 hour. Serve hot.

3   Irish Soda Bread

Although this bread is identified with the Irish it wasn't invented in Ireland. According to the Society for the Preservation of Irish Soda Bread (yes, this society really does exist) "the earliest reference to using soda ash in baking bread seems to be credited to American Indians using it to leaven their bread." Makes sense to me. One more historical note: The Irish used sour milk instead of the buttermilk in this recipe. I prefer the taste that buttermilk brings to this bread.

This bread is easy to prepare. Because it is not a yeast-bread, it only takes 15 minutes prep time. I like to slice the bread, toast it and enjoy it at breakfast with my coffee. It is also good with butter or jam (or both!). Try spreading a little peanut butter (or any nut butter) on the bread or add a slice of cheese to create an instant protein snack. It is also a wonderful complement to a good vegetarian stew.

Ingredients:
3 cups all-purpose flour (whole wheat flour also works well)
1 tablespoon baking powder
1/3 cup white sugar
1 teaspoon salt
1 teaspoon baking soda
1 egg (lightly beaten)
2 cups buttermilk
¼ cup butter (melted)

Directions:
Preheat oven to 325 degrees.

Spray a 9x5 inch loaf pan with vegetable oil and lightly dust with flour. Combine flour, baking powder, sugar, salt and baking soda. Blend egg and buttermilk together, and add all at once to the flour mixture. Mix just until moistened. Stir in butter. Pour into loaf pan.

Bake for 65 to 70 minutes, or until a toothpick inserted in the bread comes out clean. Cool on a wire rack if you have one or leave in the pan but be sure to let it cool before you slice it. Wrap in foil or plastic wrap and keep in refrigerator.

4   Mom's Popovers

Here's my mom's recipe for traditional American-style popovers. She's been gone many long years but I can still smell them as they came from the oven. My brother, John, and I ate them warm with a bit of butter and jam.

I also remember the kitchen on Minnie Street in Hayward where they were made. The kitchen was so narrow that even as a teenager I could stretch out my arms and simultaneously touch the oven on left and the refrigerator on the right. I did that only once. The wiring wasn't grounded properly so if you touched both at once you got a pretty good shock.

I was thinking of that kitchen the other day as I ordered a new gas range for our kitchen. Can't wait to make mom's popovers in my new oven. When it arrives this will be the first thing I make in her honor.

Ingredients:
2 large eggs
1 ¼ cups milk
1 tablespoons melted butter
1 cup white flour (I like to substitute ½ whole wheat for ½ of the white)
¼ teaspoon salt

Directions:
Preheat oven to 450 degrees.

Grease a muffin pan. I use my mom's heavy old cast iron pan, which is perfect for popovers.

Beat the eggs, whisk in milk and butter, and then sift in flour and salt. Whisk until smooth. Fill each muffin cup about halfway. Place popovers in the oven and bake for ten minutes. Reduce heat to 350 and bake another 25-30 minutes. Be careful not to open the oven at all while the popovers are baking.

Remove popovers from the oven and take them out of the pan. Carefully poke a hole in the top of each one to let the steam escape. Serve while still hot. I like them with butter and jam. You might also try honey. They are great with honey.

5   Peruvian Cornbread

I brought this recipe back with me when my son, Robert, and I travelled to Cuzco, Peru in 2006. We first had this bread while taking an early morning train ride down the mountains to Machu Picchu. After negotiating a couple of switchbacks, the train pulled into a small village and waited for the tourists on the train to buy food from the locals. One of the things they sold to us was this amazing corn bread. To get it, you handed a Peruvian coin out the window to the vendors. Using tongs, they plucked a 4x4 inch slice of soft, warm cornbread out of their basket and thrust it through the window.

My hope is that you enjoy this bread as much as Robert and I did.

Ingredients:
1 ½ cups boiling water
1 cup cornmeal
2 tablespoons butter (softened)
1 egg yolk
½ cup milk
½ cup cottage cheese
1 teaspoon salt
1 teaspoon baking powder
1/8 teaspoon ground allspice
1/8 teaspoon red pepper flakes
½ cup wholeto kernel corn
1 cup shredded Monterey Jack cheese
1 small onion (chopped)
1 cup flour
2 egg whites

Directions:
Preheat oven to 375 degrees.

Stir boiling water into cornmeal in a 3-quart bowl and continue stirring until smooth. Blend in egg yolk. Stir in remaining ingredients except egg whites. Beat egg whites just until soft peaks form then fold into batter. Pour into greased 2-quart casserole dish. Bake until knife inserted near the center comes out clean, 45 to 50 minutes.

6 Jalapeño Cheese Bread

I had a jones for jalapeño cheese bread the other morning and was too lazy to make a yeast bread so I created this quick bread version. I think you'll like. In addition to toasting and enjoying it with my coffee in the morning, I like to cut it into strips and serve it with a fresh garden salad for dinner.

Ingredients:
1 cup extra-sharp cheddar cheese (grated)
½ cup extra-sharp cheddar cheese (cut into quarter-inch cubes)
½ cup pepitas (toasted)
1 tablespoon fresh sage (minced)
½ cup nacho Jalapeño slices
1 ¾ cups flour
1 tablespoon baking powder
½ teaspoon salt
¼ teaspoon fresh ground black pepper
3 large eggs
1/3 cup whole milk
1/3 cup extra-virgin olive oil

Directions:
Preheat oven to 350 degrees. Generously grease an 8½ x 4½-inch loaf pan. Set aside.

Combine cheese, pepitas, sage and jalapeños in mixing bowl. Stir in flour, baking powder, salt, and pepper. Set aside.

In another mixing bowl, whisk together eggs, milk, and olive oil. Pour egg mixture over cheese/flour mixture and stir just until dry ingredients are moistened (dough will be very sticky). Transfer dough to prepared loaf pan. Spread dough evenly throughout pan.

Bake bread until golden on top and slender knife inserted into center of bread comes out clean; about 55 minutes. Remove from oven and cool bread in pan for five minutes, then turn out onto rack and cool completely.

7   Banana Nut Bread

This is a traditional nut bread recipe with bananas and flavorings thrown into the mix. It is well received by my family and friends. It makes one large loaf that is best served hot out of the oven but also freezes well if need be. Either way it is a good way to use over ripe bananas that might otherwise go to waste.

Ingredients:
1 cup white flour
1 cup whole wheat flour
1 teaspoon baking soda
¼ teaspoon salt
½ cup oil
½ cup sugar
1 teaspoon grated lemon rind
¼ teaspoon rum extract
2 eggs
2 cups ripe bananas (mashed)
½ cup walnuts (chopped)
½ cup raisins

Directions:
Mix flour, baking soda and salt. In separate bowl, mix oil, sugar, lemon rind, eggs and bananas. Combine both mixtures in large mixing bowl. Blend well. Incorporate walnuts and raisins into mixture. Pour mixture into a lightly greased loaf pan. Bake at 350 degrees for 50 minutes or until done when tested in center.

8   Oatcakes

Oatcakes are an inexpensive and nutritious snack. Substitute oat milk for cow's milk and vegetable oil for the butter and this becomes a vegan friendly recipe.

My roommate, Lol, and I made them in Berkeley and took them to class and on hikes in Tilden Park. They remind me of the biscuits the Hobbits took with them on adventures. Lembas, I think they were called.

Oatcakes are widely considered to be the national bread of Scotland, and have held that position for many centuries. They were even baked by the Romans when they occupied northern Scotland. They are made almost entirely of oats, the only cereal to flourish there at that time. Historians tell us that it was the common practice, even as far back as the fourteenth century, for the Chieftain and his followers, to carry a small sack of oatmeal strapped to the saddles of their horses when they set out on adventures.

An iron plate was also carried. This was used for the dual purpose of a shield in combat and as a cooking utensil when they made camp. A rough fireplace of stones was formed, and the oatcakes, made from oatmeal and water, were baked on the heated iron plate.

Ingredients:
½ cup milk
2 cups oats
½ cup white flour
½cup wheat flour
¼ teaspoon salt
1 teaspoon baking powder
¾ cup butter

Directions:
Preheat oven to 375 degrees.

Roll out mixture onto floured surface until ¼-inch thick. Cut into rectangles with knife or into rounds with a biscuit cutter. Place on ungreased baking sheet and bake for ten to 12 minutes.

This makes a whole bunch of lembas. Pack them up and go on an adventure!

9 Scots Scones

The origin of scones is debatable. I like to believe it comes from the Stone of Destiny (Scone) where the kings of Scotland were crowned. Scone was the name given for the Scottish bread made from oats and cooked either on an open fire or on the griddle. I had an opportunity to travel to Scotland twice and ate as many scones as possible. I also collected scone recipes. As it turns out, I could never get the recipes to taste as good as I remembered them tasting in Scotland. After many failed attempts in the kitchen I settled on this combination of ingredients, which includes oatmeal. You may cut them into any shapes you wish. Round biscuit cutters or a large drinking glass work well for shaping round scones. These are triangle shaped, golden in color and soft inside.

Ingredients:
1 ½ cups white flour
1 tablespoon baking powder
¾ teaspoon salt
¼ cup sugar
1/3 cup butter (margarine or shortening substitute nicely)
½ cup oatmeal (old fashioned...not quick oats)
¼ cup currents
2/3 cup buttermilk
Milk and confectioners' sugar

Directions:
Preheat oven to 425 degrees.

Sift together flour, baking powder, salt and sugar into bowl. This scone is not sweet. If you like a sugary scone add another tablespoon or two of sugar. Cut in butter until mixture resembles coarse crumbs. Stir in oats and currents (substitute raisins for currents?). Add buttermilk and stir until dry ingredients are just moist.

Turn out onto lightly floured surface. Fold dough and knead a couple of times then form into a 1-inch thick square. Cut into four triangles. Brush lightly with milk. Sprinkle with confectioners' sugar and place on an ungreased cookie sheet. Bake for 15 to 17 minutes or until done. Serve warm from the oven with sweet butter and jam or lemon curd.

10 Flatbread

Here's a basic flatbread recipe that's good with just about everything. I like to eat it with a hearty bowl of soup. I also use this recipe as dough for a thick-crust pizza.

Ingredients:
1 cup lukewarm water
2 1/4-ounce packages dry yeast (crumbled)
2 1/2 cups purpose flour
4 tablespoons extra-virgin olive oil
1 tablespoon coarse sea salt

Directions:
Preheat oven to 400 degrees.

Pour one cup lukewarm water into small bowl; sprinkle with yeast. Let stand until yeast dissolves, about ten minutes.

Place two cups flour in large bowl. Make well in center of flour. Pour yeast mixture into well. Using fork,stir until dough comes together. Knead in bowl, adding enough flour 1/4 cup at a time to form slightly sticky dough. Transfer to floured work surface. Knead until dough is smooth and elastic, about ten minutes. Coat bowl with one tablespoon oil. Add dough; turn to coat. Cover bowl with plastic wrap. Let stand in warm draft-free area until doubled, about 1 hour 15 minutes.

Brush a baking sheet with 1 tablespoon oil. Punch down dough. Turn out onto floured work surface and shape into 12-inch round. Transfer dough to prepared baking sheet. Cover loosely with plastic. Let rise until dough is almost doubled, about 30 minutes.

Press fingertips into dough, creating indentations. Brush with remaining two tablespoons oil. Sprinkle with salt (unless you are using this as a pizza crust). Bake until golden, about 28 minutes. Cool bread in pan for ten minutes. Remove bread from pan and serve when cool to touch.

[23 Caprese Salad]

Salads

11   Persimmon and Spinach Salad

This is a flavorful fall seasonal salad taking advantage of persimmons that are available at the farmers' market. To keep the salad fresh, assemble just prior to serving.

Ingredients:
¼ cup rice vinegar
2 tablespoons orange marmalade
1 teaspoon sesame oil
Salt and pepper
1 pound baby spinach leaves (rinsed and dried)
3 firm Fuyu persimmons (sliced into thin wedges)
¾ cup Trader Joe's Lightly Seasoned Pecans (chopped)

Directions:
In a large bowl, mix vinegar, marmalade, and sesame oil. Add salt and pepper to taste. Add spinach, persimmons, and pecans. Mix gently.

12 Edamame Salad

Our son is Robert. Early on he made it clear that he was Robert, not Bob or Bobby or Rob. Another thing he did early on was to let us know he could cook.

I like to think that because I've done the vast majority of the cooking in our family Robert saw my example and that's what got him into cooking. I'd like to think that but I would be wrong. Robert was born with a natural ability to appreciate colors, flavors and presentation when he cooks. He naturally enjoys cooking just like I do.

One of the neat things is that I have learned from him. He was the one that taught me to plate my food properly. "Dad" he said, "you eat with your eyes. Make it look good before you serve it." He was also the one that taught me to correctly pronounce Gnocchi.

Robert was cooking oatmeal (totally supervised) by the time he was in first grade. By the time he was in seventh grade he had created his own cheese enchilada recipe and was cooking it (unsupervised) for family and friends. By the time he was in high school he was preparing 4-course meals for his friends for which they were glad to pay. I was his proud sous-chef (Yes Chef! Right away Chef!) and was happy to clean up the kitchen while he sat with his friends to enjoy their company and his food.

Here's something Robert cooked for us the last time he visited from Sacramento. He prepared it from scratch after seeing something similar in a deli display and calls it Cold Edamame Salad. His recipe is loosely as follows:

Ingredients:
2 cups fresh shelled edamame (frozen is OK)
1 ½ cups corn (frozen is OK)
1 cup black beans (rinsed and drained from a 15-ounce can)
¼ cup red bell pepper (chopped)
1 tablespoon fresh cilantro (chopped)
1/3 cup lime juice
Salt and pepper to taste
1 avocado (cut into ½-inch pieces)

Directions:
Combine all ingredients except for the avocado pieces. Stir well. Add the avocados being careful not to mash them while stirring into the rest of the salad. Chill for at least 30 minutes before serving. Garnish with additional cilantro if desired.

13 Chevre Chaud Salad

This is a fun salad that is easy to prepare and looks wonderful when served. The flavors are complex and when served with a crisp white wine, help to make this salad a perfect first course for an elaborate dinner. By doubling this recipe, the salad will make a complete meal for four hungry people when served with a fresh baguette and butter.

While I'm preparing this I like to listen to one of Robben Ford's early CDs, "Talk to Your Daughter". It makes me smile and brings back good memories of the first time I prepared this for my wife, Robin, and our son Robert.

Ingredients:
5.5-ounce log fresh Chèvre cheese cut into 4 equal rounds (chilled)
¼ cup flour
½ cup Panko bread crumbs (Japanese product)
1 egg (beaten)
3 tablespoons hazelnuts (finely chopped)
2 tablespoons balsamic vinegar
¼ teaspoon Dijon mustard
1 teaspoon blackberry preserves
6 tablespoons extra-virgin olive oil
Pinch sea salt (fine)
Mixed salad greens (enough for 4 people)
Handful of candied pecans (coarsely chopped)
Handful of sun dried tomatoes (sliced into thin strips)
Salt and pepper to taste

Directions:
Preheat oven to 400 degrees.

Place flour and bread crumbs on separate plates. Beat in a separate flat bowl. Coat cheese rounds with flour. Dip cheese into egg and then into breadcrumbs. Make sure cheese is evenly coated. Place cheese on baking sheet and spoon hazelnuts on top of cheese. Gently press hazelnuts into cheese to adhere. Cover and refrigerate for ten to 15 minutes before baking (may be made the day before and refrigerated overnight).

While cheese is in the refrigerator, whisk vinegar, mustard, blackberry preserves and olive oil together in a small dish. Add a pinch of salt and whisk again. Set aside.

Bake cheese until heated through and the coating browns nicely (seven to eight minutes). Toss mixed greens with balsamic dressing. Divide greens among four plates. Top with warm cheese. Decorate salads with candied pecans and sundried tomatoes.

14 Wheat Berry Salad

This is a hearty, tasty salad served cold. The wheat berries add a chewy texture and soak up the seasonings in what is a delightful salad for all seasons. In addition to great flavor, wheat berries are inexpensive and abound in fiber. Serve on a bed of butter lettuce with fresh French bread and this is a meal in itself.

Ingredients:
1 ½ cup wheat berries (if this sounds too chewy, use ¾ cup wheat berries and ¾ cup long grain brown rice)
6 cups water
1 jar (6 ounces) marinated artichoke hearts (chopped – be sure to reserve liquid)
6 tablespoons balsamic vinegar (red wine vinegar works well if you don't like balsamic)
2 tablespoons olive oil
2 teaspoons Dijon mustard
1 teaspoon dried oregano
2 Roma tomatoes (cored, cut into ½ inch cubes)
1 cucumber (cut into ½ inch cubes)
¾ cup green onions (sliced)
1/3 cup Kalamata olives (pitted and chopped)
1/3 cup fresh mint (chopped)
¼ cup Italian parsley (chopped)
Salt and Pepper to taste

Directions:
In a four-quart pan, combine wheat berries and water. Bring to a boil. Cover and cook for approximately 35 minutes or until grains are tender. Pour into colander to drain. While still in colander, rinse briefly with cold water to arrest any further cooking. After thoroughly drained, pour into a large mixing bowl.

Drain artichoke marinade into bowl with the wheat berries. Add chopped artichokes, vinegar, olive oil, mustard and oregano to mixture. Mix well, cover and put in refrigerator to cool for at least 30 minutes.

Just prior to serving, mix tomatoes, cucumber, green onions, olives, mint and parsley into berry mixture. Add salt and pepper to taste.

15 Spicy Fava Bean Salad

Fava beans are one of the oldest known cultivated crops. Sometimes called broad beans or horse beans, they are indigenous to the Middle East and are now cultivated worldwide. When they are in season, fresh favas (and their gnarly looking bean pod) can be found at the Ojai Certified Farmers' Market. They are a wonderful addition to your diet (vegetarian or otherwise) containing a fair amount of protein, fiber, iron, potassium and vitamins A and C. If you love fresh fava beans but are tired of preparing them plain, try them in this spicy salad for a refreshing change.

Ingredients:
8 cups water
1 ½ pounds fava beans (about 2 cups when shucked)
1 tablespoon fresh epazote (chopped)
4 carrots (sliced ¼-inch thick)
½ teaspoon salt
2 medium tomatoes (chopped)
1 jalapeño chile (seeded and finely chopped)
¼ cup cilantro (chopped)
1 clove garlic (minced)
3 tablespoons lime juice
Salt and pepper to taste

Directions:
Bring the water to a boil in a large pot over high heat. Add the beans and epazote. Epazote has a dual purpose: it imparts a mild herbal flavor and helps to reduce flatulence. If you don't have it or can't find it just leave it out. No worries.

When boil begins again, cook for five minutes (no more!). Add the carrots and ½ teaspoon of salt. Cook for three to four minutes more or until the beans are just tender. Drain and rinse with cold water. The cold water retards further cooking so be sure the beans and carrots are cool before proceeding. You don't want the beans or carrots to be mushy.

Pull the skins off the beans. Transfer the beans and carrots to a medium serving bowl. Stir in the tomatoes, jalapeño peppers, cilantro, garlic and lime juice. If you like your food very spicy, try substituting Serrano chiles for the Jalapeños. If you don't want the heat at all, substitute one 4-ounce can of diced green chiles or ¼ cup diced nopale.

Toss to mix. Season with salt and pepper to taste. Chill for about an hour before serving.

16   Italian Bread Salad

When Robin made this salad for niece Annie, Annie dug into it and said "Aunt Robin...this is the best salad I've ever had!" We call it Annie's Salad.

I don't know if this will be the best salad you've ever had but I can promise it will be different. What's more, this recipe makes a bunch of salad so it's a good dish to bring to potlucks and other large gatherings.

We enjoy it as an entire meal, lunch or dinner! You can use any French bread (baguette, sour dough, whole wheat, etc.) but I like the texture and flavor of Ciabatta. In America, Ciabatta is often made with a sour dough starter called *biga* in Italy. It is the bread of choice for Panini sandwiches, which may be another reason I like it so much. Whichever bread you use, be sure to use one with a firm crust.

Ingredients:
1 loaf of Ciabatta bread (cut into 1-inch cubes)
Olive oil cooking spray
3 14-ounce cans Italian style stewed tomatoes (reserve juice)
1/3 cup Kalamata olives (chopped)
1/3 cup green bell pepper (chopped)
2 tablespoons fresh basil leaves (chopped)
1/3 cup red onion (chopped)
6 tablespoons olive oil
4 cloves garlic (sliced thinly)
3 tablespoons red wine vinegar
Parmesan cheese (freshly grated)

Directions:
Preheat oven to 425 degrees.

Lightly spray Ciabatta cubes with cooking spray and bake until brown, approximately 12 to 15 minutes. Remove from oven to cool.

Season tomatoes and juice to taste with salt and pepper. Add olives, bell pepper, basil and onions. Sauté garlic in olive oil until golden brown. Add sautéed garlic and olive oil to tomato mixture along with red wine vinegar. Place tomato mixture in refrigerator to chill.

Just prior to serving, toss bread mixture with tomato mixture. Sprinkle each serving with Parmesan cheese and serve on chilled plates.

17 Quinoa Salad

Quinoa is pronounced "keen-wah". When I journeyed to Peru a couple of years ago with our son, Robert, he and I enjoyed this traditional grain salad on the balcony of a small restaurant about an hour from Cusco at 11,000 feet in elevation.

While waiting for our food we noticed a bowl of small green leaves on our table. We were told that these "coca" leaves were a powerful stimulant and should be added to our hot tea if we had trouble acclimating to the local elevation. I tried them in my tea but our son did not. I can't say I liked the sensation.

I can say I liked the Quinoa salad they served. When we returned I tried to duplicate it and think I got close. Serve it cold on a bed of crisp bib lettuce.

Ingredients:
2 cups raw Quinoa
1/3 cup lime or lemon juice (we like it best with lemon juice although lime is traditional)
2 Aji or Serrano chiles (remove stems and seeds then chop)
½ cup olive oil
2 medium cucumbers (peeled, seeded, cut into ½ inch cubes)
2 medium tomatoes (chopped)
8 green onions (chopped – use only white part)
1/3 cup parsley (minced)
1/3 cup mint (minced)
Salt and pepper (to taste)

Directions:
Rinse the Quinoa and combine in a sauce pan with 2 quarts (plus ½ cup) water. Bring to a boil. Reduce heat and simmer for approximately ten minutes or until all the grains of Quinoa are translucent. Drain Quinoa and transfer to covered bowl. Place in refrigerator to chill for about 30 minutes.

Whisk together lime (or lemon) juice, chiles and olive oil. Set aside (be sure to wash your hands with plenty of soap and water after handling the chiles). Combine chilled Quinoa, cucumber, tomato, green onion, parsley and mint in large bowl. Mix gently. Pour juice mixture over the top of this mixture and toss to mix. Add salt and fresh ground pepper to taste.

This recipe makes a bunch of salad and will put a smile on many hungry friends at your next potluck gathering.

18 Raw Beet Salad

Beets belong to the same family as chard and spinach. Both the root and the greens are powerful cleansers and builders of the blood. Betacyanin is the phytochemical in beets that give them their rich 'amethyst' color. It is also the phytochemical that significantly reduces homocysteine levels.

Although raw beets have a wonderful flavor of their own, they are particularly tasty when marinated with orange juice and Shoyu. Shoyu is the Japanese word for soy sauce made of fermented soybeans, roasted wheat, sea salt, and koji. If you prefer a wheat-free sauce, substitute Tamari for Shoyu. Both sauces come in low-sodium versions.

Here's a simple recipe for a very tasty, nutritious raw beet salad. If you are not a raw food advocate, you can steam the beets for about ten minutes without losing too much nutrient.

Ingredients:
6 medium organic beets
2 cups fresh squeezed organic orange juice (about 6 large oranges)
2 tablespoons Shoyu or Tamari sauce (no MSG's, please!)

Directions:
Cut root tip and stalk off the beets. Do not peel. Using a clean (not soapy) green scrubbing pad, scrub outside of beets until they are clean. Thinly slice beets (here's where a good mandolin slicer comes in handy). Combine sliced beets, orange juice and Shoyu or Tamari

sauce. Let marinate for about an hour in the refrigerator before serving.

19 Fresh Carrot Salad

Wanting to know the history of carrot salad I turned to the Internet. I actually spent half an hour speed-reading recipes and various articles concerning carrots. What I found is that carrots are a basic food item in many different cultures. It seems that everyone has his or her own variation of carrot salad. My version is an easy, a fresh and a most tasty vegan raw salad.

Ingredients:
4 carrots (washed and shredded)
1 apple (peeled, cored and shredded)
1 tablespoon lemon juice
2 tablespoons agave nectar
¼ cup almonds (chopped)
Salt and pepper to taste

Directions:
In a bowl, combine the carrots, apple, lemon juice, honey, almonds, salt and pepper. Toss and chill before serving. I like to serve this on a plate of chilled, crisp lettuce.

20 Chicken-less Salad

This is a fruity, crunchy salad that is an entire meal on its own. It is also good as a sandwich filling on toasted multigrain bread or stuffed in fresh pita bread. I've even served it in a hollowed out pineapple shell as a fun salad (pineapple chunks on the side!). To spice it up you can add ½ teaspoon of curry. The curry and the fruit complement each other well.

Ingredients:
1 cup Vegenaise
2 tablespoons Dijon mustard
¼ cup chutney (Major Grey's is good)
2 ribs of celery (finely chopped)
1 cup red seedless grapes (cut in half)
2 tart apples (peeled, cored and chopped)
¼ cup fresh parsley (chopped)
Salt and Pepper to taste
2 12-ounce packages Quorn Chik'n Tenders (defrosted)
Butter lettuce
1 cup candied pecans (coarsely chopped)

Directions:
Stir together first eight ingredients (Vegenaise through salt and pepper) until well mixed. Add Chik'n Tenders and toss gently. Chill in refrigerator for approximately 30 minutes.

To serve, prepare four salad plates with a bed each of fresh butter lettuce. Spoon salad on top of lettuce and sprinkle pecans on top of salad. Consider omitting the pecans if you use this as a sandwich filling.

21 Guinness Potato Salad

The next time you see me, ask me about salads in Ireland. Totally dreadful. Really.

If you are into mayonnaise, the carrot, coleslaw and potato salads would please your tummy as they seem to be made of ½ vegetable ingredient (e.g. shredded carrots) and ½ mayonnaise. Except for one salad, my tummy was not pleased at all.

The only enjoyable salad was one that my son, Robert, found at the Guinness Storehouse Restaurant at 121 James's Street. On our last day in Dublin, Robert and I paid to take a Hop-On/Hop-Off bus tour of the city. The stop that made us hop off was on the grounds of the Guinness factory. It was here that we learned the history of Guinness beer and more importantly, how to pour a proper pint.

It was here that we also learned that not all salads are made with copious amounts of mayonnaise. I offer, for your gastronomic pleasure, the following very tasty Guinness Mustard Potato Salad recipe. It is an excellent change from Mom's traditional summer potato salad. Substitute olive oil for butter and this is vegan!

Ingredients:
6 medium potatoes
1 tablespoon onions (chopped)
1 stalk celery (chopped)
1 teaspoon salt
2 tablespoons unsalted butter(melted)
2 tablespoons unbleached flour
½ teaspoon dry mustard

1 tablespoon agave syrup
8 ounces Guinness Beer (Draft is good for this recipe)
½ teaspoon Tabasco sauce
2 tablespoons fresh parsley (chopped)

Directions:
Boil potatoes until just tender. Cool until easy to handle then peel and slice. Gently mix potatoes, onion, celery, and salt together and then set aside.

In a medium saucepan, whisk together melted butter and unbleached flour. Add mustard and sugar then slowly stir in Guinness and Tabasco sauce. Bring this mixture to a boil, stirring constantly. Just after it comes to a boil, turn off heat and pour mixture over potatoes. If you don't think potato salad is right unless it has mayonnaise, you can add a half a cup mayo at this point.

Sprinkle with parsley and toss gently. Let stand 1 hour before serving.

22 Arugula Walnut Pesto Salad

Quick and easy summer pasta recipe. 'Nuff said.

Ingredients:
12 ounces farfalle pasta
2 cups baby arugula
1 tablespoon lemon zest
1 tablespoon minced garlic
1 cup toasted walnut pieces, divided
3 tablespoons olive oil
½ teaspoon kosher salt
¼ teaspoon pepper
½ cup golden raisins

Directions:
Cook pasta according to package directions.

Whirl together arugula, zest, garlic, ¼ cup walnuts, the oil, salt, and pepper in a food processor until blended, scraping inside of bowl as needed.

Drain pasta, reserving a scant ¼ cup of the water. Return pasta to pot and add pesto, stirring to coat. Stir in remaining walnuts, the raisins and reserved pasta water. Serve with fresh French bread or crackers of your choice.

23 Caprese Salad

Our garden is starting to produce a variety of tomatoes. Here is one of our favorite ways to enjoy tomatoes fresh from the garden. Easy to prepare, a true flavor-flash on the palate and very pretty when plated.

Ingredients:
½ pound fresh mozzarella cheese (sliced ¼-inch thick)
2-3 large ripe tomatoes (sliced ¼-inch thick)
1 cup fresh basil leaves
Coarse salt and freshly ground pepper
2 tablespoons drained capers (optional)
¼ cup extra-virgin olive oil

Directions:
To prepare the salad, overlap tomatoes on a large plate. Arrange mozzarella and basil in a circular design on top of the tomatoes. Add salt and freshly ground pepper to taste. Sprinkle capers over the top. These are optional but I like the extra flavor. Caprese purists will want to leave capers off the salad.

Just before serving, drizzle an excellent olive oil (Ojai extra-virgin olive oil is good) over the salad. Serve immediately.

24 Eggplant and Bell Pepper Terrine

So what is a terrine? My online Apple dictionary defines it as: 1. a meat, fish, or vegetable mixture that has been cooked or otherwise prepared in advance and allowed to cool or set in its container; 2. A container used for such a dish, typically of an oblong shape and made of earthenware.

This recipe conforms to both definitions and is a wonderful vegan appetizer. If you're an eggplant lover, this one's for you. It takes about an hour of prep time and can be made the day before. In fact, it is best if made the day before so the terrine fully marinates. Bring it to room temperature before serving for best flavor.

Ingredients:
4 red bell peppers
2 medium eggplants (cut into ¼-inch-thick rounds)
1 small shallot (peeled and minced)
1 tablespoon balsamic vinegar
½ teaspoon salt
1/8 teaspoon black pepper
2 tablespoons extra-virgin olive oil
¼ cup organic tofu (mashed)
2 cups loosely packed fresh basil leaves
Vegetable oil cooking spray

Directions:
Roast the bell peppers under the broiler until skins begin to bubble and peel. Peppers will almost be black when they are ready. Transfer to a large baggie and close the top carefully (peppers will be plenty hot). Let steam in the baggie until cool enough to the touch –

approximately 15 minutes. Peel, seed and skin peppers. Cut into 1-inch wide strips. Set aside.

Preheat oven to 400 degrees.

Spray two baking sheets with cooking spray. Working in batches, arrange the eggplant rounds on baking sheets in a single layer. Roast until tender – about 20 to 25 minutes. Turn the rounds over after 12 minutes to ensure even cooking. Using a spatula, transfer the rounds to a wire rack to cool (wax paper works well but if you can use a rack it lets the air circulate to both sides).

In a small bowl, combine the shallot, vinegar, salt and pepper. Whisk in the olive oil until smooth. Set vinaigrette aside.

Spray a terrine with cooking spray (I use a 9x4 inch earthenware loaf pan). Arrange one-third of the eggplant rounds, slightly overlapping, to cover the bottom of the pan. Brush lightly with vinaigrette. Arrange half of the bell pepper strips, slightly overlapping, over the eggplant. Using a rubber spatula spread half of the tofu over the peppers. Top with half of the fresh basil and brush lightly with vinaigrette.

Make another layer of eggplant, vinaigrette, bell pepper, tofu and basil. Brush with vinaigrette. Top with a third layer of eggplant. Brush with vinaigrette. Using your hands, press down firmly but gently on the terrine, compressing the layers.

Cover tightly and marinate, in the refrigerator, for 12 to 24 hours. Carefully un-mold terrine onto a platter and garnish with fresh basil prior to serving.

25 Gluten-Free Tabouli

Tabouli is a Middle Eastern salad made with bulgur, tomato, cucumber and parsley. It often includes mint, onion and garlic and is seasoned with olive oil, lemon juice and salt.

This version of tabouli substitutes millet for bulgur wheat. If you've made anything with millet you know it can be mushy if cooked long enough. A short cooking time and ample rinsing give this vegan, gluten-free millet dish a fresh, tabouli like texture. Give it a try!

Ingredients:
2 teaspoons plus ¼ cup extra-virgin olive oil
1 cup millet
2 large tomatoes (diced)
2 medium cucumbers (peeled, seeded and diced)
2 bunches green onions (chopped)
½ cup cilantro (chopped)
½ cup lime juice
5–6 drops Tabasco
Salt and pepper to taste
Lettuce

Directions:
Heat two teaspoons of the oil in large saucepan over medium heat. Add millet and cook for three to four minutes, or until dry and beginning to smell fragrant. Carefully add six cups water, cover, and bring to a boil. Reduce heat to medium-low and cook for 15 minutes. Drain, rinse under cold water and drain again. Transfer millet to large bowl. Stir in tomatoes, cucumbers, green onions, cilantro, lime juice, Tabasco and remaining ¼ cup oil. Season with salt and pepper to taste and serve cold on a bed of fresh lettuce.

26 Two-Tone Coleslaw

This is a colorful, healthy, tasty and fun gluten-free vegan salad. Perfect picnic salad or side for your next BBQ.

Ingredients:
½ cup Vegenaise
3 tablespoons organic apple cider vinegar
2 tablespoons yellow onion (chopped fine)
1 teaspoon raw sugar
½ teaspoon celery seeds
3 cups green cabbage (thinly sliced)
3 cups red cabbage (thinly sliced)
½ large green bell pepper (sliced into thin strips)
½ cup carrots (peeled and coarsely grated)
1 tablespoons fresh dill (chopped)

Directions:
Whisk Vegenaise, vinegar, onion, sugar and celery seeds in large bowl. Add green and red cabbage, bell pepper, carrots, and 1 tablespoon dill. Toss to blend.

Season salad to taste with salt and pepper. Cover and refrigerate one hour. (Can be made two hours ahead. Keep refrigerated. Toss to blend before using.) Garnish salad with remaining one tablespoon dill before serve.

[33 Robin's Tortilla Soup]

Soups

27 Matzo Ball Soup

I always thought matzo ball soup was just flour dumplings in chicken soup. As a vegetarian I never tried it. I didn't understand that it is truly comfort food so for 58 years I avoided it not thinking to look for a vegetarian version.

While in Von's the other day I found myself looking at various foodstuffs including a package of Manischewitz "Matzo Ball and Soup Mix". I decided to see what ingredients went into the soup. Before I even got to the ingredients I saw a label that read "This product is lactose free and vegetarian". Reading the ingredients supported their claim. "Maybe" I said, "it's time to see what all the hoopla is about". I purchased the soup mix, jumped in the car and drove too fast through downtown Ojai.

When I got home I made the balls and the soup per instructions and waited 20 minutes for it to cook. When the timer went off I lifted the lid on the soup pan and was greeted with a wonderful aroma. The site of the matzo balls floating on top was welcoming. I knew, at that moment, that I was gonna like it.

So I thought "There's got to be a recipe out there for vegetarians". And sure enough there was but I wanted to try to make it myself. So I turned to the Internet for an introductory course on basic matzo balls.

I now know what matzo meal is all about and where to buy it. I'm told you can substitute cracker crumbs for matzo meal. That sounds reasonable but somehow it just doesn't sound right. I did substitute vegetable broth for chicken stock, which for a vegetarian, sounds spot on. There also seems to be a debate about whether the matzo balls should be floaters or sinkers. My recipe appeals to floater enthusiasts!

I added herbs as found on the Manischewitz box (but not the garlic, MSG or the monocalcium phosphate – whatever that is) and experimented until I got just the right mix of everything (it took three tries!).

Then, before you could say l'chayim, I had a wonderful vegetarian version cooking under a tight lid on my stove. Even though it is made *without* schmaltz, matzo ball soup is comfort food for sure.

Ingredients:
2 tablespoons vegetable oil
2 eggs (slightly beaten)
2 tablespoons water (ice cold)
½ cup matzo meal
¼ teaspoon salt
¼ teaspoon pepper
6 cups vegetable broth
1 teaspoon Better Than Bouillon (vegetable or mushroom base)
1 teaspoon fresh dill (chopped)
1 small carrot (grated)
Fresh flat leaf parsley for garnish

Directions:
Place first six ingredients in a large mixing bowl. Mix well. After mixing cover and refrigerate for one hour.

Fill a large pot with the broth, dill and grated carrot. Bring to a boil. After it boils, reduce to a simmer.

Take the matzo mixture out of the refrigerator and

gently make 1-inch balls by hand (be sure to wet your hands before forming balls). Slowly add the balls to the hot broth. Cover and cook on low for about 30 minutes.

Do not remove the lid during cooking! After cooking, turn off heat and remove cover. Let stand for ten minutes before serving. Garnish with parsley if desired.

28 Jalapeño Corn Chowder

Our son, Robert, and I love spicy food. Always looking for something new, we created this quick and simple soup one cold winter day last year. Fresh roasted peppers are ideal but buying them in the bottle at your favorite market works too, and keeps the prep time to less than five minutes total. To make it a true "chowder" consider breaking up soda crackers and adding them to your bowl as you sit and chow down.

Ingredients:
3 cups frozen whole kernel corn
14-ounce can vegetable broth
¼ cup roasted red peppers (sliced thin)
1 jalapeño (seeded and chopped)
1 cup half and half
¾ cup Cotija cheese
¼ cup fresh cilantro (chopped)

Directions:
In a blender, combine half of the corn and half of the broth. Cover and blend until fairly smooth. Pour into a large soup pan. Add the balance of the corn, broth and the peppers. Bring to a boil and reduce to simmer. Stir in half and half and simmer for 20 minutes to allow flavors to develop. Be careful not to let it boil after adding the half and half. Sprinkle each serving of soup with Cotija cheese and cilantro. Serve hot.

29 Baked Potato Soup

This quick and easy soup is hearty and, perhaps best of all, is a great way to use left-over baked potatoes. Although it makes a boatload of soup don't worry about leftover soup. It tastes even better the next day after the flavors have blended. Just reheat on medium heat and serve with a fresh garnish of chopped green onions.

Ingredients:
2/3 cup margarine
2/3 cup all-purpose flour
5 cups whole milk
2 cups vegetable broth
4 large baked potatoes (peeled and cubed)
4 green onions, chopped
1 ¼ cups shredded Longhorn cheese
1 cup sour cream
1 teaspoon salt
1 teaspoon ground black pepper

Directions:
In a large stock pot, melt margarine over medium heat. Whisk in flour until smooth. Gradually stir in milk and broth whisking constantly until thickened. Stir in potatoes and onions. While stirring, bring to a soft boil then reduce heat to low and cover. Simmer for ten to 12 minutes.

Mix in cheese, sour cream, salt, and pepper. Continue cooking, stirring frequently, until cheese is melted. Garnish with additional chopped green onions and a dollop of sour cream.

30 Mulligatawny Soup

I love Anna Thomas's soup recipes. Her Love Soup cookbook would be perfect if it had Mulligatawny. What's mulligatawny?

Mulligatawny is the Anglicized version of the Tamil words for "pepper water" or "pepper broth." It became popular with employees of the East India Company during colonial times in India. When they returned home, they brought the recipe back with them to England.

Mulligatawny was originally a rich curried soup made with peppers (hence the name). Over time it has gone through many variations. It is usually based on a chicken stock and curry, with cream, pieces of chicken, onion, celery, apples and almonds. Today's American version bears little resemblance to the original.

My version is vegan and gluten-free. If you can make it with all organic ingredients it is super-healthy. Substitute, for example, organic super vegetable juice for V8, use sprouted garbanzo beans instead of canned beans and organic coconut milk. However you make it, this recipe makes a whole bunch of soup. Share some with your friends and neighbors!

Ingredients:
1 tablespoon extra-virgin olive oil
4 cloves garlic (minced)
1 inch fresh ginger (grated)
2 teaspoons mild curry powder
1 teaspoon turmeric
½ teaspoon cayenne pepper
1 medium red onion (diced)

4 medium carrots (scrubbed and diced - not peeled)
1 cup fresh cauliflower florets (chopped)
2 large Granny Smith apples (peeled, cored and diced)
1 medium sweet potato (peeled and diced)
2 heaping cups thinly shredded cabbage
1 quart water
2 cups V8 vegetable juice
14-ounce can garbanzo beans (drained)
Pinch of salt
14-ounce can coconut milk (stir it thoroughly)
Juice from 1 medium lime
1 teaspoon organic gluten-free brown rice syrup (I buy mine at Rainbow Bridge)

Directions:
Combine all of the ingredients in a slow cooker except the coconut milk, lime juice and brown rice syrup. Cover and cook on high for about three hours. When the veggies are tender, add the coconut milk and lime and mix well. Add brown syrup, mix again and continue to heat on low for another 15 minutes. Garnish with shredded apple and serve hot from the pot!

Note: If you prefer a smoother texture, remove half of the soup to a blender. Puree and add back to the chunky original. Stir thoroughly before serving.

31 Leek and Potato Soup

This simple, tasty combination that has been around for a long time. Irish lore has it that leeks were one of the vegetables brought by the Normans and later the English when they came to Ireland in the 15th and 16th centuries. Adding leeks to their plain potato soup had to have been a welcome change for my ancestors.

For a vegan version, substitute vegetable oil for the butter and 2 cups more vegetable stock for the milk.

Ingredients:
4 large leeks
3 tablespoons butter
1 medium white onion (diced)
4 large russet potatoes
Heaping teaspoon salt
1 ½ quarts unsalted vegetable stock
2 cups milk
Freshly ground white pepper
Chives for garnish (snipped)

Directions:
Slice the white and pale green parts of the leeks crosswise (everything that is closer to white or yellow than green) and place in a bowl of water. Pull apart the rings and swirl to remove any dirt. Lift the leeks out of the water and drain in a colander.

Melt the butter in a soup pot over medium-low heat. Add the leeks and onion and cook, stirring occasionally, until wilted.

Peel the potatoes and cut into 1-inch cubes. Add the potatoes to the pot along with the vegetable stock. Add salt, bring to a boil, and simmer over low heat until the potatoes are tender (about 25 minutes). Remove from the stove and let cool.

Purée the soup in a blender in batches, then strain through a *coarse* sieve. Combine the soup base with the milk. Season to taste with pepper (and additional salt if needed) and reheat over moderate heat, stirring frequently. Do not let the soup boil after adding the milk.

To serve, garnish with chives and bring to the table with fresh bread, hot from the oven.

32 Lentil Soup

Lentils are the Rodney Dangerfield of vegetables. They don't get much respect.

One of the first crops cultivated by man, lentils have been a food source for over 8,000 years. Through much of that time they have been considered the food of the poor people. In ancient Greece the wealthy would never think of serving lentils to their guests or themselves. One exception was Hippocrates, the father of medicine, who prescribed lentils for his patients with liver ailments.

Lentils are most important to the diets of people in the Middle East and in India. Many Indian dishes emphasize the more than 50 varieties grown in that country.

My recipe, below, can be made with whatever lentils look good to you. I use beluga (black) lentils. The addition of lemon provides a light citrus scent to the soup. Hope you enjoy!

Ingredients:
2 cups uncooked lentils
4-5 medium potatoes (cubed but not peeled)
1 bunch Swiss Chard (chopped)
1 medium onion (chopped)
3 cloves garlic (chopped)
1 tablespoon Better Than Bouillon Vegetable Base
2 tablespoons sea salt
1 teaspoon fresh black pepper
Juice of 1 small lemon

Directions:
Put lentils and vegetables in pot and add enough water to cover. Add bouillon. Cover and cook for about two hours.

Add sea salt, pepper, lemon juice and additional water, if necessary. Simmer a few more minutes and serve hot. I like to serve this with fresh, soft dinner rolls.

33 Robin's Tortilla Soup

This is a wonderful, flavorful soup that is easy to prepare. Robin first made it in our home in Ojai and as it was simmering on the stove, the aroma made me smile. Make this soup and serve with fresh, warm tortillas or bolillo bread. Leave out the cheese and this is totally vegan!

Ingredients:
2 cups green snap beans (cut into 1-inch lengths)
2 cloves garlic (minced)
2 small zucchini (cubed)
1 medium potato (diced)
1 cup tomatillos (chopped)
14-ounce can diced tomatoes (Mexican-style is good)
1 medium onion (chopped)
1 medium bell pepper (chopped)
1 tablespoon chipotle peppers in adobo sauce (just use the sauce - not the peppers)
½ teaspoon cumin
½ teaspoon oregano
6 cups vegetable broth
½ teaspoon salt
2 tablespoons fresh lime juice
½ cup fresh cilantro (chopped)
1 cup Cotija Queso Seco (crumbled)
Tortilla Strips (lightly salted corn tortilla strips)

Directions:
Using a large pot, combine beans, garlic, zucchini, potato, tomatillos, tomatoes, onion, bell pepper, adobo sauce, cumin, oregano and vegetable broth. Bring to a boil. Reduce heat, cover and simmer for 20 minutes or more.

Remove from heat. Stir in salt, lime juice and cilantro. Garnish with Cotija cheese and tortilla strips just prior to serving.

34 Cabbage Soup

There's nothing quite like a hearty soup as summer transitions to fall and it begins cooling down in the Ojai Valley as soon as the sun sets. I like to serve this as a lite supper along with a fresh loaf of bread.

Ingredients:
2 teaspoons olive oil
1 onion (chopped)
1 garlic clove (crushed)
15-ounce can organic diced tomatoes
2 cups cabbage (chopped)
1 potato (diced)
¼ cup fresh parsley (finely chopped)
4 cups vegetable stock
15-ounce can garbanzo beans (drained and rinsed)
1 teaspoon paprika
¼ teaspoon black pepper
Salt to taste

Directions:
Heat the oil in a large pot and sauté the onion until soft, about 3 to five minutes. Add the garlic, tomatoes, cabbage, potato, parsley, stock, garbanzo beans, paprika, and black pepper. Simmer until the potato and cabbage are tender, about 15 minutes.

Ladle approximately 3 cups of the soup into a blender. Starting on a low speed, blend until smooth, making sure to hold the lid on tightly. Return the blended soup to the pot and stir to mix, adding salt to taste.

[43 Japanese Eggplant]

Fruits and Vegetables

35 Gran's Carrot Casserole

As a kid growing up in the San Francisco Bay Area, I enjoyed spending one week, just before the new school year began, at my grandmother's house in Merced. I helped Gran pick peaches off the tree in the backyard and then watched her peel and can them for use throughout the year. Although Gran wasn't a good cook I do remember one dish that I asked for every year. This was a carrot casserole she remembered her mom making for her when times were hard and all they had to eat were root vegetables stored in the cellar.

Gran's original recipe was never written down but I remember the ingredients she used. One day, when I craved her carrot casserole, I experimented until I got the right mix of ingredients. I hope you enjoy this simple dish as much as my family and I have enjoyed it over the years.

Ingredients:
1 small yellow onion (chopped fine)
½ cup butter
3 pounds carrots
¼ cup flour
1 egg
4 ounces Ritz crackers (crumbled)
¼ teaspoon salt
¼ teaspoon pepper

Directions:
Preheat oven to 350 degrees.

Sauté onion in butter until barely translucent. Take off heat and set aside. Scrub carrots. Do not peel. Cut carrots in 3 inch lengths. Steam until tender. Mash steamed carrots and add to onions. Cook over medium heat for five minutes. Transfer onion and carrot mixture to a large mixing bowl. Add flour, egg, cracker crumbs, salt and pepper. Mix well. Transfer mixture to a casserole dish or a loaf pan. Bake for approximately 1 hour. Gran served this dish with plain white rice and a fresh garden salad.

36 Idaho Potatoes

Our friend, Frances, sent this recipe from her home in Idaho. It was written on a 3x5 inch index card and had a small lapel pin attached to the card. The pin was in the shape of a potato. Very cool.

The recipe was handed down to Frances from her mom and is approximately 80 years old. What was good then is certainly good now if not even better. Frances says to be sure to use Idaho potatoes and your choice of cornflakes. Both of these ingredients make a difference in the casserole's taste.

Ingredients:
8 medium potatoes (preferably from Idaho)
1 bay leaf
1 can cream of celery soup (the original recipe calls for cream of chicken)
1 ½ cups sour cream
½ teaspoon salt
¼ teaspoon pepper
3 green onions (sliced)
2 cups cheddar cheese (grated)
½ cup corn flakes

Directions:
Preheat oven to 350 degrees.

Cook potatoes (boil in skins) with a bay leaf until barely tender. It is important not to overcook the potatoes or the consistency will be mushy. Remove bay leaf from potatoes. Cool potatoes, peel and grate coarsely (or use a ricer if you have one). Mix soup, sour cream, salt, green onions and 1½ cups of the cheese. Pour this mixture over potatoes and stir gently until just blended. Spoon into a greased 2½ quart casserole dish. Bake uncovered for 30 minutes.

Combine remaining cheese with cornflakes and sprinkle over casserole. Bake uncovered for another ten to 15 minutes and serve hot from the oven!

37 Esquites

This is a simple, flavorful Mexican dish. If you are familiar with elotes served by street vendors, you will enjoy preparing esquites at home. In Mexico, vendors cut fresh corn kernels off hot stalks as you watch. They then apply butter, herbs, chopped chiles and cheese to the corn, squeeze fresh lime over it, put it in a cup. Before you can say, "Bob's your uncle" you are wolfing it down and begging for more. Epazote is a strong Mexican herb (grows like a weed!) that is not often found in our markets. It can be purchased in dried form over the Internet or you can substitute cilantro in this recipe for the epazote. Epazote is preferred because of its mild and distinctive flavor.

Ingredients:
1 tablespoon melted butter
1 Serrano Chile (seeded, deveined and chopped fine)
1 pound fresh corn kernels
3 tablespoons fresh epazote (chopped)
¼ cup water
1 teaspoon salt
Juice from 1 fresh lime (plus additional lime wedges)
Queso Cotija for garnish (Parmesan cheese substitutes nicely for the Cotija)

Directions:
Heat butter in a saucepan over medium heat (do not burn). Add the chopped chile to the butter and sauté for two to three minutes. You may substitute a Jalapeño for the Serrano chile but either way, be sure to remove all seeds. Stir in the corn, epazote, water and salt. Reduce heat to low, cover and cook for about ten to 12 minutes. Remove from stove.

Add lime juice to the corn mixture and stir well. Serve while still hot in small bowls. Garnish with Queso Cotija and a lime wedge.

38 Rosti

Pronounced *rösti* (RAW-stee) in Switzerland, this food term means *crisp and golden*. It refers to foods, usually shredded potatoes, sautéed in butter and oil on both sides until crisp and browned, similar to our hash browns. I like to top my rosti with Queso Fresco cheese and serve it with pickled jalapeños on the side. A Swiss-Mexican infusion that works!

Ingredients:
2 medium white potatoes (grated)
2 large carrots (grated)
2 small zucchini (grated)
1 cup onion (chopped fine)
1/3 cup flour
2 cloves garlic (minced)
2 large eggs (lightly beaten)
Salt and pepper to taste
1 tablespoon butter
3 tablespoons vegetable oil
½ cup Queso Fresco (grated)
Escabeche as garnish

Directions:
Grate potatoes, carrots, and zucchini onto a clean kitchen towel. Wrap towel around vegetables and squeeze to remove excess liquid. Transfer vegetables to bowl, and stir in onion, flour, and garlic. Fold in eggs and season with salt and pepper, if desired. Set aside.

Heat butter and oil over medium heat. Take two tablespoons of Rosti mixture and form patties with your hand. Carefully lay patties in hot oil and cook two to three minutes on one side. Flip with a spatula and cook two minutes more, or until golden brown on both sides.

Serve as is or top with Queso Fresco and a garnish of escabeche on the side.

39 Boiling Onions and Raisins

Boiling onions are normal onions that are harvested when they are still young and small and tasty. They are usually found in stews but I found a way to make them stand on their own. Their pungent flavor and texture make for a wonderful side dish at Thanksgiving or as a compliment to any elaborate meal.

This dish can be made the day before and brought to the table just before sitting down to eat. And if you want to try something different, include these in your next antipasto.

Ingredients:
12 to 15 yellow or white boiling onions (1 to 2 inches in diameter)
1 ½ cups white wine
¼ cup olive oil
1/3 cup white wine vinegar
1 teaspoon thyme seeds
1 bay leaf
3 cloves garlic
1 teaspoon salt
3 tablespoons tomato paste
¼ teaspoon saffron
¾ cup white raisins

Directions:
Peel the onions being careful not to cut too much off the root end (layers will unravel). Put them in a sauce pan with the wine, olive oil, vinegar, thyme, bay leaf, garlic, and salt. If necessary, add a little water to cover.

Bring the onions to boil. Turn down the heat and simmer gently until they are almost tender. Stir in the tomato paste, saffron and raisins and continue to simmer until the onions are tender but not soft. Overcooking will make them mushy. Chill well before serving.

40 Plantains with Chipotle Dip

Plantains make for a simple and different side dish. They are known around the world as a cooking banana and although plantains resemble bananas they are longer in length, thicker skinned, and starchier in flavor. You won't enjoy peeling and eating one like you would a banana. I like to use plantains that are green to yellow in color. If they are black, they are too ripe for my tastes although you may prefer them that way.

I first enjoyed plantains at a mid-town Sacramento restaurant, Cava Latina, which featured Latin and South American food. They served their plantains with homemade habanero salsa. That salsa was so hot it was only available to regular customers and then only upon request. We serve it with our son Robert's chipotle dip, which, by comparison, is not hot at all (but it does have heat).

One final note: if you are on any kind of diet (low fat, low carbs, etc.) this is probably not the recipe to try right now. Save it for when you can afford to "splurge".

Ingredients:
3 green or green - yellow plantains
Vegetable oil for frying
1 7-ounce can Chipotle peppers in adobo sauce
½ cup sour cream
15-ounce can black beans (drained and rinsed)
Salt to taste

Plantain Directions:
Peel plantains and cut into ½ inch diagonal slices. Heat ¼-inch of oil in large frying pan over medium heat. Add plantains and cook for 4 to five minutes, turning once.

Remove from oil and place between two pieces of brown paper bag (paper towels don't work well). Roll over plantains with a rolling pin to break down fibers. The plantains should be slightly smashed. Return to oil and fry until golden brown – another three to four minutes more. Remove the plantains to paper towels (they work well here) and allow the towels to absorb the excess cooking oil while you prepare the dipping sauce.

Chipotle Dip Directions:
Remove two chilies from the can and take out seeds. Add chilies, three tablespoons adobo sauce, sour cream and ¾ cup of beans to a blender. Blend on high until creamy. Season with salt to taste. If the dip is too pepper-hot, add one tablespoon of sour cream at a time until it tastes right for you (we like it hot). This dip is best if made the night before and refrigerated allowing the flavors to blend. If making the same day, chill for one to two hours before serving.

41 Potatoes Au Gratin

Looking for comfort food loaded with carbs? Look no longer. Here's a potatoes au gratin recipe made with a vegan cheese sauce. For a change-up, add ½ cup chopped spinach to the last layer of potatoes/onions and try vegan bacon bits as a topper.

Ingredients:
2 -3 potatoes (¼-inch-thick slices)
1 onion, chopped
½ cup margarine
½ cup flour
3 ½ cups boiling water
1 ½ teaspoons salt
2 tablespoons soy sauce
1 ½ teaspoons garlic powder
¼ teaspoon dry mustard
Pinch of turmeric
¼ cup vegetable oil
¾ cup nutritional yeast
Paprika

Directions:
Preheat oven to 350 degrees.

Place potatoes and onion in pot of water, bring to a boil for ten minutes. Drain and set aside.

In a saucepan, melt margarine over low heat. Beat in flour with a whisk, continue to beat over medium heat until mixture is smooth and bubbly. Add boiling water, salt, soy sauce, garlic powder, mustard and turmeric. Beat well to dissolve the flour mixture. The sauce should cook until it thickens and bubbles. Whip in vegetable oil and nutritional yeast. Set aside.

In a casserole dish, add a layer of potatoes/onions. Spread sauce on potatoes/onions. Repeat layers until you are out of potatoes, onions and sauce. Sprinkle paprika on top. Cover and bake for 15 minutes. Uncover and bake for five minutes more.

42 Fresh Fruit Risotto

My son, Robert, and I don't get to experience risotto in most restaurants because the liquid used to flavor it is generally chicken stock. So, out of frustration, we made risotto with vegetable stock and after a few failed experiments came up with this flavorful dish. Proof positive that risotto does not need chicken stock to be ever so tasty!

Ingredients:
4-5 cups vegetable stock
4 tablespoons unsalted butter
2 tablespoons extra-virgin olive oil
1 large red onion (finely chopped)
2 Granny Smith apples (peeled, cored and chopped)
2 cups Arborio rice
1 cup dry white wine
1 large handful of red seedless grapes (cut in half)
2 small sprigs of rosemary
¾ cups Parmesan-Reggiano cheese (finely grated)
Fresh Italian parsley (chopped)

Directions:
Bring vegetable broth to a boil in a medium sauce pan. Reduce heat to simmer. Cover and allow to simmer.

Combine 2 tablespoons of the butter and all of the olive oil in a large pan and cook over medium to high heat Add onions and cook until translucent. Add apples and the rice and cook until rice is opaque. Add wine and cook until most of the liquid evaporates.

Add enough vegetable stock to this mixture to cover the rice and cook until the level of stock reduces below the level of the rice. Continue cooking and adding small amounts of stock until all of the stock is gone. Be sure to stir the rice as the stock is incorporated so that it cooks evenly. The stirring process also helps produce a more thick and creamy risotto.

Add the grapes and rosemary sprigs toward the end of cooking. Be prepared to pull the rosemary out when you feel the risotto has enough herbal flavor. You'll know the risotto is done when the rice is tender but still has a good bite.

Finish by stirring in the remaining 2 tablespoons butter and the cheese. Season with salt and pepper to taste. Sprinkle chopped parsley on top and serve hot with a chilled Italian white wine and additional grated cheese on the side.

43 Japanese Eggplant

From our garden to your table (well...from our garden to *our* table...but to *your* table via this recipe!). This simple vegan recipe takes very little time and effort to prepare. The flavor-to-effort ratio* is very high and along with a little brown rice, makes a satisfying, nutritional and calorie-conscience meal.

Ingredients:
4-5 Japanese eggplants (cut into bite-size pieces)
2 tablespoons rice vinegar
2 tablespoons vegan miso soup
1 tablespoon sugar
1 tablespoon soy sauce
2 tablespoons extra-virgin olive oil
1 teaspoon sesame oil
2 teaspoons sesame seeds

Directions:
Put a pinch of salt in a bowl of water and soak eggplants in the salted water for about ten minutes. Drain and dry them with paper towels.

Combine rice vinegar, miso, sugar, and soy sauce in a small bowl and set aside.

Heat olive oil in a skillet on medium heat. Fry eggplants for four to five minutes. Pour the sweet and sour sauce over eggplants. Cover and simmer on medium-low heat until liquid is almost gone.

To serve, add sesame oil and sprinkle with sesame seeds.

* Flavor-to-Effort ratio is something I made up. This recipe is very flavorful and takes very little effort. I would rate it an eight on my scale.

44 Root Vegetables Bake

Parsnips, rutabagas and the like are common fare in Norway. Although it may be a clumsy play on words, I call this the "back to our roots" recipe. Here's why.

My grandfather's "grandfather", Amund Eidsmoe, came to America in 1852 from Norway settling in southeastern South Dakota. It was there that my grandfather (Gramps) was born and later met and married my grandmother (Gran). Living in a home that had a root cellar with carrots, parsnips, rutabagas and potatoes was not uncommon in those days. In fact, root cellars often made it possible to eat well during the harsh winter months.

When Gran and Gramps moved to California during the Great Depression, Gran continued to cook from recipes that were passed down to her by my grandfather's side of the family. In addition to making a wonderful carrot casserole for us each fall, Gran would make this inexpensive vegetable bake at the first hint of cool weather.

Ingredients:
1 pound carrots (scrubbed and cut into ½ inch lengths)
1 pound new potatoes (quartered – scrub but no need to peel)
1 pound parsnips (peeled and cut into ½ inch lengths)
1 pound rutabaga (peeled and diced cut into ½ inch cubes)
2-3 tablespoons extra-virgin olive oil
1½ teaspoons salt
½ teaspoon pepper
1 1/3 cups cream (milk or half and half will *not* do!)
1 1/3 cups Fontina cheese

1 tablespoon parsley (chopped)
2 tablespoons finely grated Parmesan cheese
1 tablespoon breadcrumbs

Directions:
Preheat oven to 400 degrees.

Place prepared root vegetables in a large baking dish (I use a tall Corning Ware 2.8 liter dish). Drizzle with olive oil, salt and pepper. Toss to coat. Roast vegetables uncovered for 1 hour and ten minutes.

Transfer roasted vegetables to a large mixing bowl. Stir in cream, Fontina and half of the parsley. Transfer vegetable mixture back to baking dish. Sprinkle top with Parmesan cheese, breadcrumbs and balance of the parsley. Bake for another ten – 15 minutes or until bubbly. Serve hot.

45 Fenugreek Potatoes

Fenugreek (pronounced fenn-you-greek) derives its name from the Latin *Greek Hay*, illustrating its general use as cattle fodder. Today, fenugreek is used in curry powders, chutney and pickles. It is also lends a wonderful flavor to potato dishes.

Robin and I found fenugreek at BD's Earthtrine booth at the Ojai Certified Farmers' Market one crystal clear November morning. It was fresh and aromatic. I couldn't wait to get home and try it. I made a simple vegan dish using fenugreek, potatoes and plenty of tasty spices. Here's the recipe:

Ingredients:
2 medium potatoes (scrubbed and cubed)
4 tablespoons extra-virgin olive oil
1 teaspoon ground cumin
2 teaspoons ground coriander
½ teaspoon turmeric
2 teaspoons fresh ginger (minced)
2 chilies (seeded, chopped fine – jalapeños work well)
½ cup fresh fenugreek leaves (chopped fine)
salt to taste

Directions:
Scrub but do not peel potatoes. Cube and boil for about ten minutes or until not quite tender. Drain and set aside. Heat oil on medium heat. Add cumin, coriander, turmeric, ginger and chilies. Sauté for about two minutes. Add the potato cubes, fenugreek leaves and salt. Mix well and cook covered on low for about 15 minutes or until potatoes are tender and all the water from the fenugreek leaves has evaporated.

[52 Jalapeños en Escabeche]

Salsas, Spreads, and More

46 Nopale Salsa

This recipe was inspired by a conversation I had with one of the owners of Nopalito, Antonio Sanchez. I was at the Ojai Certified Farmers' Market looking at the native plants Antonio and his partners bring to the market. I mentioned that although I was vegetarian, cactus was one of the few vegetables I couldn't really enjoy. He asked why and I said "cactus and okra are just too slimy tasting for me". To which he replied "try fresh, peeled nopale that is raw. You might like it then".

The porch light in my brain clicked on! Why not experiment with cactus until I come up with something I could not only eat but would enjoy! I set out on a rainy Tuesday morning to try my luck at something simple, fresh and not slimy. The hardest part was finding fresh cactus! I finally found some at one of the wonderful Mexican food markets on Ventura Ave.

In researching cactus leaves for nutritional value I found that they are rich in vitamins A, B6, C, K. They also provide a fair amount of minerals including calcium, magnesium, potassium, manganese, iron and copper. I was excited to see if I could turn this nutritious prickly leaf into something fun to eat.

Here's what I came up with. After much trial and error I settled on a modified pico de gallo. The flavor of Olivia Chase's Chipotle Lime Salt Shake makes this salsa recipe a "keeper". If you don't have this, substitute your favorite chile powder.

Ingredients:
½ cup nopale (nopalea grande cactus - about ½ leaf - cleaned and diced*)

2 large fresh tomatoes (diced)
½ cup bell pepper (diced)½ cup white onion (diced)
¼ cup cilantro (chopped)Juice of one lime (about 3 tablespoons)
1 teaspoon Chipotle Lime Salt Shake (The Farmer and The Cook)

Directions:
Combine all of the ingredients and mix well. Refrigerate. Enjoy!

• *Here's the trick to cleaning cactus leaves. Carefully wash the leaf. Scrape the leaf to remove the tiny spines. Rinse the leaf. Take a green scrubbing pad and clean the green nubs and any remaining hair-like tiny spines from the surface. Rinse once more. Cut and dice into 3/8-inch pieces.*

47 Salsa Verde

Tomatillos are a hard, small fruit that are a bit tart, yet slightly sweet; earthy, but with a hint of citrus. In other words, like nothing else. You may have seen them in the store with their green husks and thought they were weird, green tomatoes. They are used to make mole, spicy soup and a number of other Mexican dishes. I like to use them to make vegan salsa verde. Use on enchiladas or as a condiment for any dish that needs a little extra zip!

Ingredients:
1 pound fresh tomatillos (husked and washed)
1 large yellow onion (cut into large chunks)
3 cloves garlic (peeled)
½ packed cup cilantro leaves (chopped)
½ jalapeño (de-seed if you don't like the heat)
1 tablespoon lime juice
Sea salt (to taste)

Directions:
Cut the tomatillos into quarters and put them into the bowl of a food processor. Add the onion and garlic and process until smooth. Add the cilantro, jalapeño and lime juice and process until the jalapeño is finely chopped.

Scrape the mixture into a small saucepan. Season lightly with salt and bring to a boil over medium heat. Cook, stirring occasionally, until most of the liquid is boiled off and the salsa looks like a fine relish - about 15 minutes. Cool before using.

Note: The sauce can be refrigerated for up to 1 week. If refrigerated, you may want to add a little salt and/or lime juice to taste before serving.

48 Magic Oatmeal

Kids love this. It is a quick but hearty and nutritious breakfast perfectly measured out for one person. Double the recipe for two helpings. Add fresh blueberries as a topping if you have them!

Ingredients:
½ cup quick oats
½ cup boiling water
1 tablespoon peanut butter
1 teaspoon organic Sucanat (or organic brown sugar)
1 tablespoon wheat germ
½ ripe banana (sliced)
½ cup oat milk (room temperature)

Directions:
Put oats, water, peanut butter, and brown sugar in a bowl and stir together until water is absorbed and oats are soft. Stir in wheat germ. Top with sliced banana and oat milk.

Note: I use regular oats, cooking them per box instructions. When they are ready (about five minutes) I stir in the peanut butter, Sucanat and wheat germ.

49 Vodka Sauce

Our son, Robert, first served this at a dinner he prepared for his friends at our home in Northern California. Full credit goes to Robert for an easy and tasty sauce recipe. I like it over ravioli, but it is equally good with penne, linguini, gnocchi or another pasta of your choosing.

Ingredients:
2 tablespoon butter
1 tablespoon olive oil
1 medium onion (chopped)
28-ounce can Italian plum tomatoes (drained, seeded and chopped)
1 ½ cups heavy cream
1/3 cup vodka
½ teaspoon dried crushed red pepper flakes
Salt and pepper (to taste)

Directions:
Melt butter and olive oil in saucepan over medium-low heat. Add chopped onions and sauté for about six minutes or until translucent. Add tomatoes and reduce until almost no liquid remains in pan - 20 to 25 minutes. Be sure to stir frequently.

Add cream, vodka, and red pepper flakes. Cook for another two minutes on low heat. Season to taste with salt and pepper.

50 Pico de Gallo

I just finished harvesting baby green onions from Robin's garden. Yes, she knows I was out there. In fact, she asked if I'd help her by digging these up early so she could use the soil for cucumber plants that need more room than the small cups they started in as seeds.

As soon as I washed the green onions, I began to think of what I could use them in. At the moment I was jonesing for chips and dip. So I found an old Pico de Gallo recipe and modified it slightly to accommodate the green onions.

I used our baby green onions along with cilantro fresh from our herb garden and tomatoes, onions, garlic and peppers fresh from the Ojai Certified Farmers' Market. Here's the recipe. Just combine all of the ingredients in a large mixing bowl, stir and enjoy!

Ingredients:
5 to 6 medium tomatoes (diced)
1 medium white onion (diced)
¼ cup fresh cilantro (chopped fine)
2 small serrano chilies (seeded and chopped fine)
1 garlic clove (minced)
juice of 1 lime
10 baby green onions (chopped)
salt to taste

51 Chow Chow

If you have a vegetable garden, there is nothing better than picking fresh bell peppers, cucumbers, red onions and tomatoes for this recipe. My dad would bring tomatoes, peppers and onions into the house and as he was chopping them you could literally taste the vegetables by taking a deep breath through your nose.

For the cucumbers, dad would buy regular green waxy-skin cucumbers at the store. I use Armenian and lemon cucumbers and the chow chow is still awesome. In addition to the vegetables, my dad added salad oil, vinegar, salt and pepper.

For me, this is the taste of summer and takes me back to my childhood on a lazy summer day in the San Francisco Bay Area. Why my dad called this chow-chow I don't remember. Now that I think about it, it does not call for pickling as does southern style chow chow found just about anywhere south of the Mason-Dixon line.

Ingredients:
2 medium cucumbers (diced)
2 small red onions (diced)
2 medium bell peppers (diced)
2 large tomatoes (diced)
1/3 cup salad oil
¼ cup red wine vinegar
salt
pepper

Directions:
Combine diced veggies with salad oil and vinegar. Add salt and pepper to taste. To spice it up a bit you can add a small, diced Serrano chile (without seeds of course!).

This tastes best when chilled for about an hour before serving. It is a good side dish at barbecues (yes – vegetarians *can* grill).

That's it. Easy to make so make a boatload and share it with friends!

52 Jalapeños en Escabeche

Escabeche is typically a Mediterranean cuisine, which generally refers to a dish of poached or fried fish that is marinated in an acidic mixture before serving. In addition to Mediterranean countries, escabeche is common in Salvadoran, Panamanian, Peruvian, Philippine, Puerto Rican, Dominican, Guatemalan and Mexican cuisine.

And although escabeche is generally identified with fish dishes, it also refers to the vegan marinade itself. In Mexico, sliced or whole jalapeños en escabeche are used as a garnish for a variety of dishes.

Here's my vegan recipe and my directions for making jalapeños en escabeche.

Ingredients:
16 ounces jalapeño peppers
1/3 cup olive oil
2-3 medium white or yellow onions (thickly sliced)
3 medium carrots (scrubbed and thickly sliced)
1 head garlic (cloves separated and peeled)
4 cups apple cider vinegar
1 cup water
2 tablespoons Kosher salt or sea salt
2 bay leaves
½ teaspoon dried oregano
4 sprigs of fresh marjoram or ¼ teaspoon dried
4 sprigs of fresh thyme or ¼ teaspoon dried
1 tablespoon sugar

Directions:
Wash the chilies, leaving the stems intact. Cut a cross in the tip end of each chile so that the vinegar will be able to penetrate.

Heat oil in a large, deep skillet. Add the chilies, onions, carrots, and garlic. Fry over medium heat for about ten minutes, turning them over occasionally.

Add the vinegar, water, salt, herbs, and sugar and bring to a boil. Lower the heat and simmer for ten minutes. Make sure the chilies are entirely cooked through before canning.

Pack four pint-sized sterilized jars with the chilies and vegetables. Top with the vinegar and seal. Process in a hot water bath for ten minutes. Share with friends and family.

53 Hachiya Smoothie

Have you heard of the Hachiya persimmon? I hadn't until I stopped in at the Friend's Ranch Packing House on Maricopa Highway. Emily Ayala and her dad, Tony Thacher, were busy packing tangerines for sale at local farmer's markets. I saw a couple of persimmons on a table but didn't ask about them. I was more interested in the tangerines at the time. When I left, Emily offered me one of the persimmons saying it was a Hachiya.

Wanting to know more about this variety of persimmon, I turned to the Internet. Here's what I found after a couple of hours of careful research. There are two basic kinds of persimmons: Fuyu and Hachiya. Fuyu are hard and ripen on the tree. They are ready to eat as soon as picked. Hachiya are not ready to eat off the tree unless you like a high pucker factor once you bite in. They must be allowed to ripen, usually in a bowl, until they are soft and kind of squishy.

When I asked Tony how to eat a ripe Hachiya, he replied "my grandmother used to eat them with a spoon". I was tempted to eat the Hachiya as soon as I got home but I promised Emily I would create a unique recipe with the one she gave to me.

I've eaten persimmon cookies, persimmon cake and had sliced persimmon fruit in salads. To create a truly unique recipe took some out of the box thinking. Here's what I came up with. It is a nutritious, easy-to-make persimmon breakfast smoothie recipe and was created for Emily and her dad, Tony, to enjoy this winter:

Ingredients:
1 ripe Hachiya persimmon (kinda squishy like a water

balloon)
1 tablespoon Ojai Valley honey
1 container (5.3 oz) Greek style nonfat vanilla yogurt (vanilla does not mask the delicate apricot-like flavor of the Hachiya)
¼ teaspoon powdered ginger (use more if you like)
½ cup fresh Friend's orange juice

Directions:
Remove stem and calyx (the small pulpy middle where the seeds are) from the persimmon. Don't worry about the peel. Leave it on. Puree in a blender. Add remaining ingredients and mix until smooth. Change it up by increasing the orange juice to ¾ cup and adding half a peeled banana. Um, um good!

54 Middle Eastern Dip

Pita bread is a staple in Middle Eastern food. Garlic, walnuts, cumin, lemon juice and olive oil are staple ingredients in Middle Eastern recipes. Spices such as black pepper and paprika, among others, are found in a Middle East spice blend called baharat.

So why do I mention this? Because this Middle Eastern recipe has them all. When blended together, they make a dip that is a favorite of friends and family whenever I serve it. Although it is neither quick nor easy to make, the extra effort is worth it. I like to make this the night before so the flavors have a chance to mellow and blend.

Ingredients:
3 red bell peppers (about a pound or so)
1 six-inch pita bread
1 cup water
1 garlic clove
¾ cup walnut pieces
1 ½ teaspoons paprika
¾ teaspoon ground cumin
1 tablespoon balsamic vinegar
1 tablespoon fresh lemon juice
2 tablespoons extra-virgin olive oil
¾ teaspoon coarse ground salt
Black pepper to taste

Directions:
Roast the bell peppers under the broiler until skins begin to bubble and peel. Peppers will almost be black when they are ready. Transfer to a deep bowl and cover with plastic wrap (or place in a large zip-lock baggie). Let steam until cool enough to the touch –

approximately 15 minutes. Peel, seed and skin peppers. Set aside.

Toast Pita bread until crisp and golden. Break into 2-inch pieces; place in a bowl and cover with water. Soak until soft, about ten minutes. Transfer to a sieve and drain well, pressing out excess water. Set aside.

Combine garlic and walnut pieces in a food processor. Process until fine crumbs form – about ten seconds. Add paprika, cumin, peppers and pita bread. Process until smooth – about ten to 12 seconds. Add vinegar, lemon juice, olive oil, salt and pepper. Pulse until combined.

Transfer to a serving bowl and cover with plastic wrap. Refrigerate at least one hour before serving. Drizzle a little olive oil on top, sprinkle lightly with paprika and bring to room temperature before serving. Serve with additional toasted pita bread (cut into triangles) or crackers.

55 Welsh Rarebit

Whether you call it Welsh rabbit or Welsh rarebit the Welsh do love their toast and cheese. But, then, so do the Irish, the Scots and the Brits.

Eighteenth-century English cookbooks reveal that *rabbit* was considered to be a luscious supper or tavern dish, based on fine cheddar-type cheeses and wheat breads, which were central to English cuisine.

Carried to the New World by colonists, it survived through most of the nineteenth-century in its many forms with such names as Toasted Cheese or Yorkshire Golden Buck. By the late 1800s it had achieved elevated status as *rarebit*, one of the period's fashionable and often pretentious chafing dish presentations.

When made at home, the American version often resembled an open-faced, melted cheese sandwich. This version harkens back to the original recipe taking advantage of sharp cheddar cheese and fine porter beer.

The type of beer you use makes all the difference. The Welsh prefer porter but the Irish in me prefers Guinness. If you like stout beer, consider making this with Guinness Extra Stout.

Ingredients:
2 tablespoons unsalted butter
2 tablespoons all-purpose flour
1 teaspoon Dijon mustard
1 teaspoon vegan Worcestershire sauce
½ teaspoon salt
½ teaspoon freshly ground black pepper
½ cup porter beer

¾ cup heavy cream
1 ½ cups sharp cheddar cheese (shredded)
2 drops hot sauce
4 slices toasted multigrain bread (Les Bles D'Or brand is excellent)

Directions:
In a medium saucepan over low heat, melt the butter and whisk in the flour. Cook, whisking constantly for two to three minutes, being careful not to brown the flour. Whisk in mustard, Worcestershire sauce, salt, and pepper until smooth. Add beer and whisk to combine. Pour in cream and whisk until well combined and smooth. Gradually add cheese, stirring constantly, until cheese melts and sauce is smooth; this will take four to five minutes. Add hot sauce. Pour over toast and serve immediately.

56 Knishes

Knish is a Ukrainian word meaning dumpling. Knishes were developed by Eastern European Jews who brought knish, and other favorite recipes, with them as they emigrated from Europe. One historical account says "Knishes were made at home until Yonah Schimmel, a rabbi from Romania, began to sell them at Coney Island in New York City, and also from a pushcart on the Lower East Side."

The rabbi would have made his knishes with eggs and butter. If you are vegan and celebrate the Festival of Lights, give this vegan version a try.

Ingredients:
3 russet potatoes (peeled and chopped)
1 large onion (peeled and chopped)
2 cups vegetable broth
¼ cup plain soymilk
2 tablespoons fresh extra-virgin olive oil
Salt and pepper to taste
4 whole wheat tortillas
Dijon mustard

Directions
Preheat oven to 350 degrees.

Boil potatoes and onions in the water or stock until potatoes are soft (ten to 15 minutes).

Remove potatoes and onions from the water with a slotted spoon, reserving the cooking water. Add the soymilk, olive oil, salt and pepper, and mash with a fork or potato masher until sticky. If you need more liquid, add the potato cooking water, one teaspoon at a time.

The end result should be a lumpy mixture.

Lay tortillas flat and spread mustard onto each one. Drop about two tablespoons of the potato mixture in the middle of the tortilla and spread in a line from left to right. Fold the tortillas like a burrito using additional potatoes to seal it shut at both ends.

Place knishes with the folded side down on a baking sheet. Spread a little more mustard on the top of each knish. Bake for about ten to 15 minutes, or until the tortilla is firm but not crisp. Cool before eating.

57 Roasted Red Pepper Sauce

My friend, Vicky, came over to the house the other day lugging a large box. I hurried out to the porch to lighten her load. "I have all these peppers left over after making a wonderful spaghetti sauce", she said. "Would you be able to use the left over peppers before they spoil?" I accepted the box from her and replied, "Would I? You bet I would". What a great community we live in.

I actually had other plans for that morning but when one is given a gift such as this...well, I rose to the challenge. Although I roasted and used all of this super-ripe mix of peppers, here's how I specifically used some of the sweet peppers:

Ingredients:
6 to 8 whole sweet peppers (or 4 bell peppers)
2 tablespoons pine nuts (roasted)
2 tablespoons olive oil
½ medium onion (finely diced)
8 cloves garlic (roasted)
½ cup heavy cream
Fresh Parmesan cheese
Salt and pepper to taste

Directions:
Roast peppers on a grill or under the broiler until skins begin to bubble and peel. Peppers will almost be all black when they are ready. Transfer to a large baggie and close the top carefully (peppers will be plenty hot). Let them steam in the baggie until cool enough to the touch – approximately 15 minutes. Peel, seed and skin peppers. Using a blender, puree peppers with pine nuts. Set aside.

In a skillet or pot over medium heat, drizzle in olive oil. Add onions and garlic and cook until onions are translucent. Pour in pepper puree and stir together. Reduce heat to medium low and pour in cream. Stir to combine and add salt and pepper to taste.

58 Pimiento Cheese Spread

I remember mom purchasing Kraft pimiento cheese spread when I was a kid. It was a treat for her and a treat for my brother and me when she spread it on bread and shared it. Unfortunately the glass container it came in was so small that by the time she shared with us, there wasn't much left for her.

Here's my recipe for pimiento cheese spread and it makes a whole bunch of spread. Share it with your family, friends and neighbors!

Ingredients:
3 ounces longhorn cheese (grated)
3 ounces extra-sharp white cheddar cheese (grated)
4-ounce jar pimientos (drained)
¼ cup Vegenaise
¼ teaspoon celery salt

Directions:
Mix all ingredients in large bowl. Cover; chill. Transfer dip to serving bowl. Surround with baguette slices and vegetables.

59 Vegetarian Gravy

Gravy has been around for centuries and takes many forms. As a kid, I remember my mom cooking a pot roast and just before serving the roast, whisking flour into the fatty juice to make a quick gravy. But what do you do if you don't eat meat? How do you make a tasty gravy without meat juices? Just keep reading!

This is an excellent vegan gravy that tastes good on mashed potatoes, biscuits or on your favorite vegetarian "loaf". It is much tastier than the gravy packets found at the local grocery store and is a healthy alternative to fatty gravies as it has very little cholesterol content. The key ingredient in this recipe is nutritional yeast. It provides a robust flavor and can be found in bulk at most health stores. I found it locally at Rainbow Bridge and The Farmer and The Cook.

Ingredients:
½ cup vegetable oil
1/3 cup onion (chopped)
5 cloves garlic (minced)
½ cup flour (whole wheat works well but unbleached is good too)
4 teaspoons nutritional yeast
4 tablespoons Tamari sauce
3 ½ cups vegetable broth
½ teaspoon dried sage
Salt and pepper to taste

Directions:
Heat oil in a medium saucepan over medium heat. Sauté onion and garlic until soft and translucent (about five minutes). Stir in flour, nutritional yeast and Tamari sauce. Form a smooth paste. Gradually whisk in the broth. Season

with sage, salt and pepper. Go light on the salt, as the Tamari and nutritional yeast are naturally salty. Bring to a boil and immediately reduce heat to simmer, stirring constantly until thickened.

This recipe makes a boatload of savory gravory!

60 Shallot Vinaigrette

Choosing the right shallot to bring home from the Farmers' market is similar to choosing the right onion. Choose ones that are firm and heavy for their size, and have dry skins with no sprouting. In fact, shallots are very similar in taste to onions with a hot taste when eaten raw and a more delicate flavor when cooked. Cooking shallots brings out a hint of garlic flavor. Although this recipe is based on fresh uncooked shallots, I think you'll enjoy the nice blend of flavors.

Ingredients:
2 tablespoons fresh shallots (chopped fine)
2 teaspoons Dijon mustard
2 tablespoons red vinegar
½ teaspoon salt
¼ teaspoon pepper
6 tablespoons olive oil
1 tablespoon lemon juice
1 tablespoon Greek yogurt

Directions:
Add first 5 ingredients to a blender. Blend until smooth. With blender running, add oil and continue to blend until creamy. Add lemon juice and then the yogurt. Pulse blend a couple of times until yogurt is incorporated.

That's it! Refrigerate and enjoy.

61 Rice Cakes with Habanero Sauce

Here's a gluten free vegan appetizer that is not only nutritious but also pleasing to the palate. The rice cakes can be made with either white or brown rice – your choice. The sauce is made with one of the hottest peppers in the world so please use half of a Habanero pepper. If the capsicum in this pepper is a little too much for your palate, substitute a Jalapeño. Habaneros are measured at 300,000 Scoville Heat Units (SHUs). Jalapeño peppers are measured at 3,000 SHUs or 100 times less "hot". No matter which pepper you choose, be sure to seed it first, wash your hands with soap and water and *then* continue preparation.

Ingredients:
Extra-virgin olive oil (for brushing pans and rice cakes)
½ cup cilantro leaves
½ cup water
2 cups cooked long grain rice
½ cup canned bamboo shoots (drained and chopped fine)
1 teaspoon salt
2 tablespoon additional olive oil (for sauce)
½ cup shallots (diced fine)
½ habanero pepper (seeded and minced)
1 teaspoon sweet paprika
½ teaspoon dried thyme
½ teaspoon ground allspice
½ teaspoon ground cloves
2/3 cup fresh orange juice
1/3 cup fresh lime juice
1 teaspoon agave nectar
Salt and pepper to taste
Butter lettuce
¼ cup chopped fresh mint for garnish

Directions:

To make Rice Cakes: Brush 9x9-inch baking pan (or glass dish) with olive oil. Purée cilantro with ½ cup water in blender or food processor. Combine cilantro purée, rice, bamboo shoots, and salt in bowl. Press rice mixture into prepared baking dish. Cover with parchment or wax paper and weigh down placing a second baking dish on top filled with cans. Cool at room temperature for at least two hours.

Heat oven on high broil. Brush baking sheet with olive oil. Cut rice into 12 squares. Place squares on baking sheet brushing a little olive oil on top of each. Put in oven and broil until well browned on top (about six to seven minutes in my oven). Remove from oven. Turn squares over and brush a little more olive oil on the bottom sides. Return to oven and broil the bottom side for another four to five minutes. Remove from oven and set aside.

To make Habanero Sauce: Heat olive oil in saucepan over medium-high heat. Sauté shallots for approximately eight minutes. Add habanero, paprika, thyme, allspice, and cloves. Sauté for another 20 to 30 seconds. Add orange juice, lime juice, and agave. Simmer for ten to 15 minutes. Sauce should be reduced but not thick. Season with salt and pepper. Set aside.

To serve: Place rice squares on a bed of butter lettuce. Drizzle sauce over each rice cake, garnish with a sprig of fresh mint and serve while sauce is still warm.

62 Lo-Cal Potato Salad

This is a potato-less potato salad. An oxymoron you say? Well, maybe. But once you make this and serve it to family and friends you *and* they will be believers. Makes me wonder if the secret to a good potato salad is not the potatoes as much as the creamy sauce. You be the judge and let me know how this compares to mainstream potato salad.

Ingredients:
1 large head cauliflower (florets only)
½ envelope ranch dressing/dip mix
1½ cups Vegenaise
½ cup sour cream
3 tablespoons Dijon mustard
¼ teaspoon salt
2 tablespoons milk
1 cup red onion (diced)
2 celery stalks (diced)
3 tablespoons seasoned rice vinegar
4 hardboiled eggs (chilled and chopped)
¼ cup chives (chopped)
2 tablespoons fresh dill (chopped)
2 tablespoons parsley (chopped)
Paprika (for garnish)

Directions:
Place cauliflower in a large microwave-safe bowl and pour 1/3 cup water over it. Cover and microwave for six to eight minutes (until cauliflower is soft). Once cool enough to handle, drain excess water from the cooked cauliflower. Lightly mash two cups of the cauliflower and place in a blender. Add milk and puree or pulse until blended. (Don't worry if it isn't completely

smooth.) Spoon into the blender and mix until creamy. Set aside.

In a medium bowl, mix together the ranch mix, Vegenaise, sour cream, mustard and salt. Chop the balance of the cauliflower into small half-inch pieces. Place cauliflower pieces in the bowl and add the onion, celery and vinegar. Toss and let stand for five minutes.

Pour the blender mixture over the vegetable mixture and stir to incorporate. Fold in the chopped eggs, chives, dill and parsley. Chill for a couple of hours to allow flavors to blend.

Sprinkle with paprika and serve cold.

63 Ojai Mojo

In the Canary Islands, a Spanish archipelago located 100 km west of Morocco, *mojos* or sauces are made with oil and vinegar and served cold as an accompaniment to potatoes, meat and fish. Mojos can be red or green and are sometimes spicy. Cilantro gives this mojo an intense flavor and deep green color, but it's not spicy at all. To spice it up, add one seeded, finely chopped jalapeño chile.

Ingredients:
2-3 garlic cloves (peeled)
1 large bunch cilantro (Trim off stems)
¼ teaspoon ground cumin
½ teaspoon coarse salt
½ cup extra-virgin olive oil
4-5 tablespoons water
Lemon juice to taste

Directions:
Peel the garlic cloves and trim stems from the cilantro.

Process the garlic, cilantro, cumin and salt in a blender to create a paste. While blending, drizzle olive oil in gradually. Add small amounts of water until the sauce is thick, but not as thick as a paste. Add one to two teaspoons lemon juice or more, according to your taste. You can use vinegar as they do in Spain but give this a try first. Serve at room temperature.

Dog Biscuits

Time to retire our 28 year old dog biscuit cutters and buy new ones. The ones we are using now are all worn out. The final biscuit looks more like small "Blobs" than biscuits in the shape of dog bones. Even the round tin that the biscuit cutters came in is showing signs of aging.

We make the biscuits below on a regular basis for both dog and for human consumption. They are vegetarian *and* they are good for you! Just make sure you have a glass (or bowl) of water nearby. Eating these dry is like eating a bag of Saltine crackers without something to drink. Here's our tried and true recipe for dog biscuits:

Ingredients:
4 cups whole wheat flour
½ cup corn meal
1 teaspoon garlic powder
1 teaspoon onion powder
1 egg
2 tablespoons vegetable oil
1 ¾ cups water

Directions:
Preheat oven to 325 degrees.

Combine flour, corn meal, garlic powder and onion powder. Mix to incorporate. Make a well in the center of the flour mixture and add the egg, vegetable oil and water to the well. Again, mix to incorporate. The mixture may need additional water to form. If so, add one teaspoon at a time until the dough forms into a ball. Knead by hand.

Roll out until dough is ½ inch thick. Cut into dog bone shapes (or any other shape). Put cut out bones on a baking sheet and bake for approximately 50 minutes. Let cool before giving them to your pooch (or snacking on one yourself).

This recipe makes enough biscuits for you, for your dog and for your dog's friends!

65 Citrusy Kumquat Chutney

Have an abundance of kumquats out on the tree and you're afraid to pick them because you don't know what to do once they're in the house? Try this fresh, citrusy kumquat chutney. It can be prepared up to two weeks ahead of time.

Ingredients:
2 cups chopped tree-ripened kumquats
1 cup organic sugar
¾ cup fresh Ojai blood-orange juice
½ cup dried cranberries
¼ cup chopped shallots
1 tablespoon plus 1 teaspoon fresh ginger (finely minced)
¼ teaspoon ground pepper
¼ teaspoon aniseed (chopped)
¼ teaspoon ground cinnamon
1/8 teaspoon ground cloves

Directions:
Wash kumquats and quarter lengthwise. Remove seeds and pulp.

Combine all ingredients in heavy medium saucepan. Bring mixture to boil. Reduce to medium high heat and cook, stirring occasionally, for about ten minutes or until kumquat skins are tender and mixture thickens. Transfer chutney to bowl and let cool. Cover and store in refrigerator until ready to use.

66 Simple Lettuce Wraps

This is an easy and inexpensive snack, appetizer or midday meal. They can be a little messy so be sure to have plenty of napkins available as you slam them down. The spicy dipping sauce is a recipe that works well with the lettuce wraps as well as a variety of other Asian foods.

Wrap Ingredients:
1/3 cup cornstarch
1/3 cup flour
¼ cup brown sugar
16 ounces organic extra firm tofu (cut into ½ inch dice)
3 tablespoons vegetable oil
3 garlic cloves (minced)
1 cup mushrooms – shiitake are good (diced)
½ cup cashews (chopped)
¼ cup hoisin sauce
1 head iceberg or butter lettuce

Spicy Dipping Sauce Ingredients:
¼ cup sugar
½ cup water
2 tablespoons soy sauce
2 tablespoons rice wine vinegar
2 tablespoons hoisin sauce
1 tablespoon lemon juice
1/8 teaspoon sesame oil
1 tablespoon prepared hot mustard
2 teaspoons hot water
1 teaspoon red chile garlic sauce

Wrap Directions:
Using a large baggie, mix cornstarch, flour, and brown sugar. Add tofu and toss to coat.

Using a frying pan, heat oil over medium high heat. Carefully add coated tofu to pan. As it starts to brown, add garlic, mushrooms, and cashews. Cook for about five to six minutes, then add hoisin sauce. Cook for additional two minutes to glaze the tofu.

Peel off as many leaves of lettuce as you want to make lettuce wraps and then add one more. These can be addictive. Spoon tofu mixture into lettuce leaves and wrap one side of the leaf over the other. Serve with the dipping sauce below.

Spicy Dipping Sauce Directions:
Using a small bowl, dissolve sugar in water. Add soy sauce, rice wine vinegar, hoisin sauce, lemon juice and sesame oil. Mix well. Set aside.

Combine the hot water with the hot mustard and mix until combined. Add chile garlic sauce to mustard mixture. Set aside.

Combine first mixture with mustard/chile sauce. Mix well. Refrigerate until ready to use.

67 Guacamole

Here is a simple, tasty and nutritional raw-food vegan recipe for guacamole that Robin and I thoroughly enjoy every time we make it:

Ingredients:
4 ripe avocados
2 tablespoons red onion (chopped fine)
3 tablespoons fresh cilantro (chopped)
½ teaspoon fresh garlic (crushed)
2 tablespoons lime juice
¼ teaspoon sea salt
1 jalapeño or serrano chile (seeded and chopped fine)

Directions:
Place all ingredients in a large flat-bottomed mixing bowl. Using a potato masher/blender, mash all ingredients together. Stir well. Cover and refrigerate prior to serving.

68 Mushroom and Garlic Tapas

The word tapas means "cover" in Spanish. Tapas were invented in Andalusia, which is in the south of Spain. In this wine-making region, it is the custom to place a saucer on top of a glass of wine in order to keep the little fruit flies out. A small amount of food placed on top of the saucer helped attract clients to the wine bar.

In some tapas bars, Spanish champiñones al ajillo are served in small, shallow bowls along with toothpicks. I serve these garlicky mushrooms as an appetizer with plenty of crusty bread to sop up the delicious juices.

Ingredients:
1 tablespoon + ½ teaspoon extra-virgin olive oil
5 cloves garlic (peeled and sliced)
20 large *fresh* white button mushrooms (cleaned and quartered)
1 tablespoon flour
½ cup vegetable broth
½ cup dry sherry
¼ teaspoon red pepper flakes
2 tablespoons chopped parsley

Directions:
Heat one tablespoon of oil in skillet over low heat. Add garlic, and cook one minute or until transparent. Add mushrooms, and cook ten minutes without stirring. Remove mushrooms and garlic from the pan and set aside.

To the pan, add the ½ teaspoon of oil and the flour and cook for approximately one minute, stirring constantly. Slowly whisk in broth and sherry and cook until the roux is smooth. Return the mushrooms and garlic to the pan, add the parsley and pepper flakes and cook for another two minutes, or until flavors blend. Season with salt and pepper, if desired, and serve hot.

69 Sundried Tomatoes and Eggplant Spread

If the eggplant we get from our local market is neither oval in shape nor white like an egg…why is it called an eggplant? According to the website "Bite Size of Amazing Facts" the first eggplants to reach European chefs during the Middle Ages were a rare white species, oval in shape. They did, indeed, resemble an egg and therefore the name "eggplant" was born and perpetuated even when other varieties (including oblong purple ones) made their appearance.

The best thing, I think, about eggplants is the nutritive value. Eggplants are low in calories, provide a fair amount of protein and fiber and are relatively low in carbohydrates. The good news is they contain no fat or cholesterol! The really good news is that when combined with sundried tomatoes, roasted garlic and fresh herbs…the overall flavor is amazing!!

Ingredients:
2 pounds eggplant
1/3 cup extra-virgin olive oil
4 large cloves roasted garlic (chopped)
½ cup oil-packed sun dried tomatoes (chopped)
½ cup fresh flat-leaf parsley (chopped)
½ cup fresh basil (chopped)
Juice of 1 lemon
Salt to taste
Pinch cayenne pepper

Directions:
Peel the eggplant and cut into 1-inch cubes. Sauté the eggplant in the olive oil until tender – about 15 or 20 minutes on medium heat. This is a lot of eggplant to cook so unless you have a gigantic frying or sauté pan it

will take two batches to cook it all. If you do it in two batches, use three tablespoons olive oil for the first batch and three tablespoons for the second. The eggplant will soak up the olive oil as it cooks. Not to worry. We want the eggplant to soak it up. It adds flavor.

When the eggplant is cool, combine the balance of the ingredients with the eggplant and blend them together. I like to use a blender on pulse but mashing by hand works well too. Again, this is a lot of eggplant. It will take a few trips to the blender to get it all mashed up. If using a blender, be sure to pour all blended ingredients into a large bowl and then mix the batches together until all ingredients are well blended.

I like to refrigerate this for about an hour before serving (but it is not necessary). Use as a spread on crostini or use as a dip with your favorite cracker.

[Herb garden 3 steps outside the kitchen door.]

The Goodness of Fresh Herbs

Basil (Pesto)

Whether going to seed or still productive, our small herb garden boasts nine different fresh herbs. We grow basil, tarragon, oregano, thyme, rosemary, chives, parsley, mint and epazote. We planted cilantro but it didn't do well. Savory is in there but it didn't last long. Gotta work on that next year.

One of the herbs that grows best for us is basil. Although there are a number of different varieties of basil (as with most herbs) we grow sweet basil (O. basilicum).

Sweet basil is most commonly associated with Italian cuisine although it is native to Asia and is used extensively in Thai cuisine. Most of the Italian dishes I make with tomatoes include basil and it is the essential ingredient in pesto. We make a bunch of pesto at a time and freeze it. Basil freezes well but it does not refrigerate well. To keep it fresh in the refrigerator you can place the sprigs in water but only for a couple of days at the most.

Here's a basic recipe for pesto:

Ingredients:
2 cups (packed) fresh basil leaves
½ cup extra-virgin olive oil
3 tablespoons pine nuts
3 garlic cloves (pressed)

Directions:
Place 1 cup basil leaves in food processor on "chop". Add ½ the nuts and garlic and chop again briefly. Slowly add ¼ cup of the olive oil stopping to scrape down the sides of the container. Set food processor to blend until it

forms a smooth paste. Repeat until all ingredients are used.

71 Tarragon (Creamy Dressing)

Although American cuisine does not favor tarragon, it is a major flavoring in French cuisine including béarnaise sauce and fines herbs. The French call it the "King of Herbs".

The ancient Greeks reportedly used it as a remedy for toothaches. Today, we know that tarragon contains an anesthetic chemical, eugenol, which figures prominently in anesthetic clove oil. See the movie Marathon Man for a disturbing use of clove oil as an anesthetic. On second thought, even though Dustin Hoffman is amazing in his role as Babe, skip the movie! It is disturbing.

Tarragon loses potency as it dries. This may be one reason it is frequently preserved in vinegar, which captures its essence and provides tastiness when used in salad dressings. But why purchase tarragon vinegar when you can enjoy fresh tarragon from your garden?

Here's a creamy salad dressing recipe using fresh tarragon (we also use it as a dip for steamed artichokes):

Ingredients:
½ cup Vegenaise
¼ cup salad oil
1 tablespoon lemon juice
1 tablespoon white wine vinegar
1 teaspoon soy sauce
¼ teaspoon pepper
1 clove garlic (minced)
1 ½ tablespoons fresh tarragon (minced)

Directions:
In a small bowl, whisk Vegenaise, oil, lemon juice, vinegar, soy sauce, pepper and garlic. Add tarragon and mix well. Cover and chill for a couple of hours to allow tarragon's goodness to infuse the dressing.

72 Oregano (Chilaquiles)

The use of oregano can be traced back to the ancient Greeks. Its botanic name is Origanum vulgare, Greek for "joy of the mountains". It is said to have been invented by the goddess Aphrodite who gave it to man to make his life happy. Newly married couples were crowned with wreaths made of oregano. It was also put on graves to give peace to the newly departed. In Great Britain, oregano was an additive to snuff (a pulverized, dry tobacco concoction taken through the nose).

Although oregano is an important ingredient in Mediterranean cooking, its use was little known in the United States prior to the Second World War. Soldiers discovered its flavor and aroma during the Italian Campaign and brought it back with them. I say "many thanks" to those that did!

Although oregano is commonly associated with Italian cuisine, it is an important ingredient in Mexican cuisine as well. Mexican oregano has a stronger, more bitter flavor than its Greek cousin and therefore holds up better to the stronger flavors in dishes such as albondigas soup, pollo con oregano and for us vegetarians, chilaquiles .

Here's my recipe for chilaquiles:

Ingredients:
15 6-inch corn tortillas (cut into strips)
8 plum tomatoes
12 tomatillos (remove husks)
1 medium white onion (chopped)
2 jalapeño chilies (remove stems)
6 cloves garlic (peeled)

2 ¼ teaspoons dried Mexican oregano
1 ½ teaspoons black peppercorns
3 sprigs fresh thyme
1 bay leaf
4 cups cilantro leaves
6 large egg whites (beaten)
2 ounces Queso Fresco (grated)
Sour cream
Avocado (sliced)

Directions
Preheat oven to 350 degrees.

Line two baking sheets with parchment paper. Spread tortilla strips in single layer on baking sheets. Spray with cooking spray, flip, and spray other side. Bake seven to ten minutes, turning once, or until crispy. Set aside to cool. Note: This step can be eliminated by substituting store bought "tortilla strips".

Place four tomatoes, six tomatillos, ¾ cup onion, one jalapeño, three cloves garlic, oregano, peppercorns, thyme, and bay leaf in large pot; cover with three cups water. Bring to a boil over medium-high heat, and simmer 15 minutes, or until tomatoes are soft and tomatillos are pale. Remove bay leaf and set aside.

Preheat oven to broil. Spread remaining four tomatoes, six tomatillos, ¾ cup onion, jalapeño, and three cloves garlic on baking sheet. Broil 25 minutes, or until vegetables are browned, turning occasionally. Cool slightly.

Transfer broiled vegetables to pot with boiled vegetables and stir in cilantro. Blend in batches in blender until smooth. (You should have about nine cups). Transfer blended sauce to a large cooking pot and bring to a boil. Reduce heat to low and simmer for 15 minutes or until sauce is slightly thickened.

Increase heat to medium-high. When sauce boils, turn off heat. Fold in egg whites. Add Queso Fresco and the tortilla strips. Toss gently to coat strips.

Adjust oven temperature to 375 degrees. Spread completed chilaquiles into a greased baking dish (I use a 2.8 liter Corning Ware dish). Cover and bake ten minutes, or until tortillas have absorbed most of sauce. Remove from oven and let stand, uncovered, for five minutes. Serve at the table with individual dishes of sour cream, sliced avocado and Queso Fresco to use as toppings.

73 Thyme (Cream Cheese Spread)

Thyme (Thymus vulgaris) is a member of the Mint family. I know! Doesn't smell or taste like mint at all!! My herb garden features two of the 100+ varieties: garden thyme and lemon thyme. There is a noticeable difference in the flavor and aroma of each.

The noun Thyme comes from the Greek word "thymos" meaning spirit or smoke. The Romans were reported to have bathed in it before going into battle to gain vigor, strength and courage. In the Middle Ages, Knights would have their Lady embroider a sprig of thyme on their scarves as a sign of bravery.

Ancient Sumerian texts show that thyme was used as an antiseptic. Today thyme is widely used in aromatherapy and mouthwashes such as Listerine. Bees are attracted to thyme and favor it for making honey. Insects, however, are repelled!

Some folks make a cup of thyme tea, put it in a plant mister, and spray the doorways and window sills in the summer to keep insects from entering the house. I've tried it and it works for me!

Here's a simple recipe using fresh lemon thyme:

Ingredients:
8 ounces Cream Cheese
1 tablespoon fresh lemon thyme (chopped)
1 tablespoon fresh parsley (chopped)
½ teaspoon garlic (crushed)

Directions:
Blend all ingredients thoroughly and roll into a 1" diameter log. Cover with wax paper and refrigerate overnight. When ready to serve, slice into 1/4" rounds and serve on crackers.

74 Rosemary (Pasta Sauce)

Rosemary is an aromatic, woody shrub which comes from the Mediterranean, where it can be found everywhere from the hillsides of Provence to the ruined temples of Greece. The word "rosemary" comes from the Latin ros maris, "dew of the sea". In Italy it still grows abundantly along the coastline. In my garden I keep it trimmed so as not to get out of hand.

Rosemary is thought to be the herb of romance and fidelity. The Romans used it as an aphrodisiac. Young maidens would slip sprigs of rosemary into their pillowcases so that their true love would come to them in their dreams. Today, in addition to cooking, rosemary is extensively used by horticulturalists as a decorative and aromatic hedge.

Here's another use for rosemary. After bathing our dog Willow, we make a doggie body tea using rosemary and apple cider vinegar. It is a soothing rinse for her skin and helps to keep insects away.

Better yet, here's a simple pasta sauce using fresh rosemary from the garden:

Ingredients:
2 tablespoons extra-virgin olive oil
1 medium onion (chopped)
¼ cup celery (chopped)
1 large carrot (chopped fine)
4 ounces fresh mushrooms (sliced)
3 cloves garlic (minced)
1 tablespoon cup fresh rosemary leaves (chopped)
¼ teaspoon salt
¼ teaspoon black pepper

¼ teaspoon sugar
28 ounce can crushed tomatoes (retain liquid)
2 tablespoons tomato paste

Directions:
Add olive oil, onions, celery and carrots to a large sauce pan on medium heat. Stirring occasionally, Cook until onions are translucent; about five minutes. Add mushrooms, garlic, rosemary, salt, pepper and sugar and continue to cook for an additional five minutes. Add crushed tomatoes (and their liquid) and tomato paste. Stir well.

Cover sauce and simmer for one to two hours so flavors will blend. Stir periodically. If sauce thickens too much while cooking add water, ¼ cup at a time, to bring to proper consistency.

75 Chives (Vegetable Dip)

Chives are native to Asia and Eastern Europe although they are grown in almost all areas of the northern hemisphere today. Like many of our words for herbs, "chive" comes to us from the Latin "cepa". It also comes from the French "cive" (Old French). The first recorded use for the world in English was around 1400. Suffice it to say that chives have been enjoyed for a long, long time!

According to the website indepthinfo.com, the first recorded use occurred in China about 3000 B.C. Marco Polo is credited with bringing chives from China to Europe. The gypsies of ancient times used chives in fortune telling. It was believed that you should hang bunches of dried chives around your house to ward off disease but then, they also thought that hanging garlic cloves around your neck warded off vampires.

Ancient Romans believed chives could relieve the pain from sunburn or a sore throat. Chives are believed to be a good source of calcium and can improve digestion as well as high blood pressure.

Here's a refreshing dip recipe using chives snipped fresh from the garden:

Ingredients:
1 cup Vegenaise
1 cup sour cream
1 tablespoon lemon juice
2 teaspoons fresh chives (chopped)
1 teaspoon garlic salt
½ teaspoon dill weed
½ teaspoon paprika

Directions:

Combine all ingredients. Refrigerate for at least 2 hours before serving with carrot sticks, cucumber sticks, celery, etc. Best if refrigerated overnight so flavors blend. Garnish with additional chopped chives just before serving.

76 Parsley (Brown Rice)

Parsley is a member of the Carrot family and gets a bum rap as a garnish at restaurants such as Denny's, Carrows, IHOP, et al. I was told, as a kid, that I should eat my parsley because it would help keep my breath fresh. Like I cared whether I had fresh breath at 7 years of age. As I matured, I found that the chlorophyll in parsley actually does help to prevent bad breath.

Parsley has not always been a garnish used in plating food. The ancient Romans describe two types of parsley in fourth century B.C.: one with dense, crowded leaves and the other with open, broader leaves. I'm thinking the latter is probably what we call Italian parsley. Many chefs favor Italian parsley, P. neapolitanum, as it is sweeter than standard curly leaf parsley, is more flavorful and it is easier to chop. It is, in fact, the most popular and widely used culinary herb in the world.

So when was it first used as a garnish? According to the World's Healthiest Foods website, "the ancient Greeks held parsley to be sacred, using it to not only adorn victors of athletic contests, but also for decorating the tombs of the deceased". I'm thinking Alexander the Great would be upset at its casual use as a garnish today.

Here's a brown rice recipe using fresh parsley:

Ingredients:
2 teaspoons olive oil
1 medium onion (chopped)
1 cup brown rice
2 ½ cups vegetable broth
1 cup fresh parsley (chopped)

¼ cup sliced unsalted almonds (roasted)
Salt and pepper to taste

Directions:
Heat the oil in a medium saucepan over medium-high heat. Add the onion and cook, stirring occasionally, until soft, about six minutes. Stir in the rice and cook for one minute. Add the broth and bring to a boil. Reduce heat and simmer, covered, until the rice is tender and the broth is absorbed, 25 to 30 minutes. Stir in the parsley and almonds. Add salt and pepper to taste.

77 Mint (Iced Tea)

The herb mint belongs to a large family with over thirty species. We grow two kinds of mint in our garden: spearmint and chocolate. Both have unique flavors and aromas. I prefer spearmint because of its taste and versatility. I use chocolate mint in a wonderfully rich mint-chocolate mousse.

Mint is native to the Mediterranean and western Asia. All mints have the volatile oil menthol, which gives it that characteristic cool taste. The ancient Greeks believed mint could clear the voice and cure hiccups. Early American immigrants brought mint with them for its medicinal properties but it was also a symbol of hospitality in the south. Southern ladies and gentlemen would rock in chairs on their "verandas" sipping Mint Juleps. My first taste (literally) of southern hospitality was served by my friend, Steve Morrison, on his patio in Chula Vista as we celebrated the nation's 200th anniversary with my Uncle Bob and Aunt Elaine. Steve was born in Georgia and knew how to make the perfect Julep.

Here's a simple, refreshing iced tea recipe using your choice of fresh mint:

Ingredients:
3 ounces fresh ginger (not peeled; sliced)
6 cups water
1 cup mint leaves
6 bags green tea
½ cup honey (may substitute blue agave sweetener)
2 tablespoons lemon juice

Directions:

In a large saucepan over high heat, combine the ginger and water and bring to a boil. Remove from heat and add the mint and tea bags. Cover and let steep for 15 minutes. Strain the liquid into a large pitcher or other container. Stir in honey and lemon juice. Chill in the refrigerator.

Epazote (Black Beans)

Epazote is an herb that grows wild in Mexico and throughout Central and South America. It grows wild in my herb garden, as well, and I am glad. It has a strong, unique flavor that when used judiciously, is a welcome addition to my cooking arsenal!

This strong herb has been used for hundreds of years in Mexican cuisine dating back to the Aztecs who not only used it in cooking but also for medicinal purposes. The name actually comes from the Aztec word *epazotl*.

In the Yucatan epazote is used to expel intestinal worms and to act as a mild laxative. Freshly uprooted green plants thrown into fires helps to drive away mosquitoes and flies. It can also drive away people and is known as skunk weed (not to be confused with poor quality marijuana) in North America because of its pungent smell.

One more thing: epazote is not only super flavorful but acts as a natural "Beeno" when added to beans or other gas producing vegetable dishes.

Here's a black bean recipe using the herb epazote:

Ingredients:
16 ounces uncooked black beans
6 cups water
2 cloves garlic (chopped fine)
1 small onion (chopped)
1 serrano chile (seeded and chopped fine)
1 teaspoon cumin
1 sprig epazote (finely chopped)
salt to taste

Directions:
Rinse beans. Put beans and water in a large pot and bring to a boil. Reduce heat to low, cover the pot and simmer for about 2 hours. Add all other ingredients and simmer for another hour or until beans are tender.

[81 Vegetarian Meatballs]

Hearty Entrees

79 Valley Vegetarian Burger

What's all this brouhaha about the best vegetarian burger in the Ojai Valley? Everyone knows it's the Valley Vegetarian Burger. So why even look elsewhere. Can't say it's super-healthy but it is nutritious. Most of all it's *tasty*. The combination of zesty guacamole, extra sharp cheddar cheese, blue cheese, red onion and roasted red pepper is a perfect complement to the vegan Grillers.

Here's my signature Valley Vegetarian Burger recipe with grilled cheese sandwiches in place of hamburger buns. Seriously satisfying! Be sure to have a stack of napkins on hand while eating.

Ingredients:
1 red bell pepper
4 slices American cheese
4 slices whole-grain sandwich bread
3-4 tablespoons butter
3 ounces blue cheese (crumbled)
1/3 cup guacamole
3 ounces aged white cheddar cheese (grated)
1 slice red onion (¼-inch thick slice)
2 Morningstar Grillers

Directions:
Trim stem from bell pepper, cut in half and remove veins and seeds. Grill for approximately seven minutes or until skin blackens and peels. Turn over and grill for another four minutes. Set aside.

Butter one side of all four slices of bread. Place two slices of American cheese between two slices of buttered bread and place on grill – butter side down. Repeat for remaining bread and American cheese. Grill cheese sandwiches until they are gently browned on each side.

Heat Grillers in a microwave on high for two minutes.

To assemble, crumble blue cheese on top of one of the grilled cheese sandwiches. Place one of the grillers on the blue cheese and spread guacamole on top of the griller. Place the second griller on top of the guacamole. Place the cheddar cheese on top of this griller followed by the roasted red pepper and the thick slice of red onion. Top with remaining grilled cheese sandwich and serve while still warm.

80 Nutty Meatloaf

How can you make a vegetarian dish that is "meaty"? Try this recipe. I think you'll be surprised. Nut loaf recipes became popular in the United States during World War I when meat was scarce. They became popular again when food was rationed during World War II.

This is a recipe I have served over the last 25 years to the enjoyment of my meat eating friends. I like to cut a ¾ inch slice off the finished loaf and make "meat loaf" sandwiches using this recipe. Whether you use it as an entrée or as sandwich filling, this nutty loaf is a tasty alternative to the traditional "meat loaf".

Ingredients:
1½ cups walnuts
½ cup cashews or almonds
2 tablespoons unsalted butter
1 yellow onion (finally chopped)
2 teaspoons minced garlic
1½ cups cooked brown rice (it works with white but brown is tastier)
2 tablespoons parsley (chopped)
1 tablespoon fresh marjoram (chopped)
2 tablespoons fresh thyme (chopped)
1 teaspoon fresh sage leaves (chopped)
4 eggs (beaten - Egg Beaters work well)
12 ounces Gruyere cheese (grated)
1 cup cottage cheese
1 teaspoon salt
½ teaspoon freshly ground black pepper

Directions:
Heat oven to 350 degrees. Grease a 9½ x 4½ x 2½ inch loaf pan (you can use shortening, cooking oil or butter). A round 9-inch spring form pan works well also. Set aside.

Toast walnuts and cashews on a baking sheet until lightly browned, about ten minutes. Do not burn. Let cool. Finely chop and set aside (I use a blender to chop the nuts).

Increase oven temperature to 375 degrees.

Melt butter in a saucepan over medium heat. Add onion and garlic. Cook until translucent, about three minutes. Transfer to a large bowl and add toasted nuts, rice, parsley, marjoram, thyme, sage, eggs, Gruyere, cottage cheese, salt and pepper. Mix well.

Pour mixture into prepared pan and bake until golden brown and firm to the touch, about 50 to 55 minutes. Serve with mashed potatoes and gravy and fresh baked bread.

81 Vegetarian Meatballs

You might very well ask whether a veggie meatball is an oxymoron. I would answer yes to that. I would also add that their hearty texture and rich taste are actually preferred over real meatballs by most of my meat-eating friends.

This recipe takes some planning ahead as the balls need to be frozen before they bake. Your efforts, however, will be well worth it. Serve these as a main course with rice or with whole-wheat noodles. I like them served over thin spaghetti. They can also be served alongside turkey at Thanksgiving and other celebrations to the delight of everyone.

Ingredients:

Meatballs:
2 ½ cups cracker crumbs
1 ½ cups ground walnuts
1 teaspoon season salt
3 teaspoons sage
1 large onion (chopped fine)
1 ½ cups Longhorn cheese (grated)
6 tablespoons parsley (minced)
8 eggs
Pinch of garlic powder

Sauce:
1 bunch green onions (chopped)
1 clove garlic (crushed)
1 tablespoon butter (margarine substitutes nicely)
2 cans mushroom soup
16 ounces sour cream

Directions:
Preheat oven to 350 degrees.

Mix together cracker crumbs, walnuts, seasonings, onion, cheese, parsley, eggs and garlic powder. Form into balls approximately 1½ inches in diameter. Place balls on baking sheet and freeze overnight - or make them in the morning, freeze and take out at dinnertime.

Sauté green onions and garlic in butter. Add soup and sour cream. Set aside.

Place balls in baking dish and pour sauce over frozen balls. Cover with foil and bake for 45 minutes. Serve "bubbling" hot.

82 Lemongrass Tofu

Fresh lemongrass is easily found in the Ojai Valley markets and its aroma, along with the flavor of Hoisin sauce and sate chile paste, will delight your friends and family. This dish is a nice starter for an elaborate dinner or enjoyed as a nutritious lunch time meal. Steamed brown rice is a nice complement if you want a complete, nutritious dinner.

Ingredients:
16 ounces medium firm organic tofu (cut into 1-inch cubes)
4 cups canola oil
¼ cup organic Tamari
¼ cup white vinegar
¼ cup granulated organic sugar
1 tablespoon Hoisin sauce
3 tablespoons water
3 tablespoons vegetable oil
1 small yellow or white onion (¼-inch thick slices)
1 tablespoon garlic (minced)
1/3 cup fresh lemongrass (cut off the lower bulb - remove tough, outer leaves and use a food processor to grind the remaining yellow stalk)
1 tablespoon sate chile paste (buy some in the store or make it yourself*)
½ cup fresh shitake mushrooms (remove stems – slice ¼-inch thick)
2 stalks green onion (chopped)
2 tablespoons natural rice vinegar
Fresh cilantro for garnish

Directions:
Heat 4 cups of oil in a 2-quart saucepan over medium-high heat. Cut tofu into 1-inch squares and pat dry with

paper towels to absorb excess water. Fry tofu cubes until golden brown. Drain on a paper towel (this step can skipped if you buy store-bought deep fried tofu and cut it into 1-inch pieces) and set aside.

Mix tamari, vinegar, sugar, Hoisin sauce and water together in a small bowl. Set aside.

Heat a wok or large skillet over high to medium-high heat until very hot. Add 3 tablespoon vegetable oil. Add onion, garlic and lemongrass. Sauté for 30 – 40 seconds. Add chile paste and tamari mixture (see set aside above). Stir until incorporated.

Add tofu to the wok or skillet. Stir or toss all ingredients together until the sauce coats all. Add mushrooms and green onions. Deglaze with rice vinegar and continue to stir fry until the mushrooms are cooked through (about two minutes).

Garnish with a few sprigs of cilantro and serve immediately.

* Sate Chile Paste
Ingredients:
1 teaspoon crushed red chile pepper
¼ cup organic peanut butter
½ cup organic extra-virgin olive oil
4 garlic cloves minced
1 tsp curry

Directions:
Mix crushed chile pepper and peanut butter together. Set aside. Heat the oil on medium and cook the garlic to release the fragrance and oils. Add in the remaining ingredients along with the pepper/peanut butter

mixture. This will start to foam and them form a paste. Remove and let cool. Refrigerate until you are ready to use. The paste will keep for up to a week in the refer.

83 California Dreamin' Burger

I first made this for my wife, Robin, one cold winter day while listening to an old Mamas and Papas tune. I wanted to make something different that would brighten her spirits. I wanted something fun and unusual. And although this unusual non-beef burger was concocted in a small northern California town where we lived at the time, it will still keep you safe and warm in Ojai.

For those of you who are new to fennel I think you'll like it. It can be found at the Ojai Certified Farmers' Market and provides a mild flavor that complements the Portobello mushrooms, bell peppers and pesto. Ciabatta bread substitutes nicely for focaccia if you like a more sturdy base for your burger.

As John Phillips might have said to Michelle one cold day in New York, California dreamin' on such a winter's day!

Ingredients:
1 yellow bell pepper
1 red bell pepper
2-3 tablespoons olive oil
1 fennel bulb (trimmed and thinly sliced – Still available at the Farmer's Market)
4 large Portobello mushrooms
4 4-inch squares focaccia bread (cut in half horizontally)
½ cup prepared pesto sauce
2 ounces blue cheese (thinly sliced)
½ cup marinated sun-dried tomatoes (cut into thin slivers)

Directions:

Preheat oven on high broil. Grill bell peppers until blackened on all sides, turning occasionally. Place peppers in a large bowl and cover with plastic wrap. Let stand until peppers are cool enough to handle (about 20 minutes). Remove skins, seeds and ribs. Cut peppers into strips. Set aside. Leave oven on broil.

In a large frying pan, heat 1 tablespoon olive oil and grill fennel slices for 2 to three minutes on each side or until lightly browned and tender. Set aside with peppers. Clean and de-stem Portobello mushrooms. Brush on both sides with remaining olive oil. Grill two to four minutes per side or until tender.

Place focaccia (cut sides up) in oven and broil until nicely toasted. Spread cut sides with pesto sauce. Place mushrooms on bottom halves of focaccia and top with blue cheese, sun-dried tomatoes, peppers and fennel. Replace focaccia tops pesto side down and serve while hot.

84 Tofu Frittata

This is a spicy vegan recipe that takes advantage of the firmness of organic tofu as a substitute for eggs. Great snack food for kids of all ages.

Ingredients:
1 pound organic extra firm tofu
1 tablespoon extra-virgin olive oil
2 fresh asparagus spears (chopped)
¼ cup onion (diced)
¼ cup chunky salsa (drained of excess liquid)
1 teaspoon turmeric
10 black olives (sliced)
1 tablespoon nutritional yeast
Salt and pepper to taste

Directions:
Preheat oven to 375 degrees.

Drain tofu. Slice in half so you end up with two squares about ½ inch high. Press between paper towels until most of the excess moisture is absorbed. Crumble tofu into a bowl and set aside.

Heat olive oil on medium heat. Sauté asparagus for about two to three minutes. Add onion and continue to sauté for a minute or two. Add salsa and turmeric. Continue cooking until liquid starts evaporating (doesn't take long!). Add the olives. Continue heating until almost all of the liquid is gone and everything seems tender but not mushy. Add this mixture to the crumbled tofu and mix in nutritional yeast.

Press mixture into a casserole dish or pie pan and bake for about 30 minutes. Once the top is brown and firm and the middle doesn't jiggle, call it done. Serve warm or cold. Your choice. I like it best after it has been refrigerated for about an hour.

85 Irish Fondue

I told a friend the other day that I made a wonderful Irish Fondue for St. Patrick's Day. He came back with, "Irish Fondue? The Irish don't have fondue".

"Any culture that has wonderful cheeses, including the Irish, have a fondue of sorts", I replied. "It doesn't need to be Swiss. In fact, a good fondue doesn't need Emmenthaler or Gruyere cheese. It doesn't need kirsch. You just need a proper recipe".

"Prove it", he said with a twinkle in his eye.

That's when I knew he had maneuvered me into making my much appreciated Irish version of Swiss Fondue. Here's what I made:

Ingredients:
1 stick (8 tablespoons) unsalted Irish butter (room temperature)
½ teaspoon dry mustard
½ teaspoon garlic (minced)
12 slices firm-textured bread (crusts removed)
8 ounces Kerrygold Blarney cheese (shredded)
¾ teaspoon fresh chives (chopped)
½ teaspoon Vegetarian Worcestershire sauce
salt and fresh ground pepper to taste
4 eggs
1 ½ cups, milk
2/3 cup dry white wine
2/3 cup heavy cream

Directions:
In a small bowl, blend together the butter, mustard, and garlic. Spread an equal portion of the butter mixture on

each slice of bread. Fit 6 slices of the bread, buttered-side down, into the bottom of a 9-by-13-inch baking pan or glass dish (reserving the remaining buttered bread for the top of the casserole).

In a small bowl, stir together the cheese, chives, Worcestershire sauce and the salt and pepper. Sprinkle this cheese mixture over the bread in the baking dish. Place the remaining bread, buttered-side up, on top of the cheese.

In a medium bowl, whisk together the eggs, milk and wine until well blended. Pour the mixture over the bread and cheese composition in the baking dish. Allow the casserole to stand for 30 minutes. Pour the cream over the top. Cover tightly with plastic wrap and refrigerate for at least 12 hours. You might be tempted to put this in the oven right away but please don't. Letting it refrigerate is important to get the flavor and texture just right.

Preheat the oven to 350 degrees. Bake the casserole, uncovered, until lightly browned and set - 60 to 70 minutes. Remove from oven and allow the casserole to rest for 15 minutes. Cut into finger-sized strips (or as desired) and serve hot.

Tip: Make a day ahead and keep refrigerated until ready to bake.

86 Mexican Hominy Bake

If you have never tried or never enjoyed hominy, give this a shot. This is easy, quick to prepare and nutritious. It can be a meal in itself or a hearty side dish.

I use Mexican style white hominy because it is large, flavorful and is processed by cooking in limewater. This process is called nixtamal and removes the germ and the hard outer hull from the kernels making them more palatable and tastier than the American process, which soaks the kernels in lye. It is thought that the nixtamal process increases the nutritional value of the hominy. It definitely improves the flavor and aroma.

You can substitute American style hominy if you want but try this recipe with Mexican style hominy at least once!

Ingredients:
1 29-ounce can Mexican style white hominy (drained)
¼ cup onion (chopped)
¾ cup sour cream
1 cup Jack cheese (shredded)
4-ounce can green chilies
Salt and pepper to taste

Directions:
Preheat oven to 350 degrees.

Mix all ingredients and pour mixture into a small casserole dish. Bake uncovered for 40 to 45 minutes (how much easier could this be!). Serve while still hot. I serve this dish with a fresh garden salad.

87 Broccoli-Ricotta Cheese Pie

If you are like me, you probably thought ricotta cheese to be uninteresting. Before being put off by the idea of yet another recipe for using bland ricotta cheese, read on. This one has flavor!

The trick to cooking with ricotta is knowing what to blend it with. This recipe adds tender broccoli florets and just the right amount of herbs to give this pie a wonderfully savory goodness. Let me know how you like it!

Ingredients:
1 tablespoon extra-virgin olive oil
½ cup white onion (chopped)
2½ cups broccoli florets (blanched)
1 tablespoon fresh basil (chopped)
¼ teaspoon fennel seed (crushed)
¼ teaspoon salt
1 cup ricotta cheese
2 large eggs (beaten)
2 teaspoons milk
1 tablespoon grated Parmesan cheese
2 refrigerated pie crust dough sticks

Directions:
Preheat oven to 350 degrees.

To blanch broccoli florets bring a large pot of salted water to a boil. Add broccoli to boiling water and cook for 1½ to two minutes (until slightly cooked through and tender). Carefully remove broccoli from water by draining in a colander and set aside to cool.

In a large skillet, add olive oil and onion and cook over

medium high heat for three to four minutes stirring occasionally. Reduce heat to medium and stir in broccoli, basil, fennel and salt. Cook for an additional four to five minutes. Remove from heat and set aside.

In a large mixing bowl, combine ricotta, eggs, milk and Parmesan cheese. Add broccoli to this mixture and set aside.

Spray a 9-inch spring form pan with cooking spray. Roll out one stick of pie dough and line bottom and ¾ up the side of the pan with dough. Spoon the broccoli-ricotta mixture into the crust. Roll out and tuck the remaining dough stick down inside the pan, pinching to join and seal with side dough. Cut slits in top with knife.

Bake 50 to 55 minutes or until golden brown. Remove from oven and let cool for 15 minutes. Unmold and serve warm or refrigerate and serve later.

88 Sprouted Burger

There are many veggie burger recipes but our vegetarian son, Robert, and I prefer this one made with sprouted garbanzo beans. We made them during his visit over the holidays. Fresh, sprouted beans provide a number of micronutrients and are high in dietary fiber. They are also well known for being rich in iron. One cup, for example, provides 25% of your average daily iron needs.

If you can't find sprouted beans you can substitute two cans of organic store bought beans. Make these two or three days ahead of time, store covered in the refrigerator and cook when you need them for a quick, nutritious meal. For a change, make them 2½ to 3 inches in diameter and serve on a fresh mini bagel instead of a regular hamburger bun.

Ingredients:
2½ cups sprouted garbanzo beans (I like Ojai Valley Sprouts at the farmers' market)
Vegan egg replacer (equivalent of 4 large eggs)
½ teaspoon Farmer and Cook Lime Salt Shake (or substitute sea salt)
1/3 cup fresh cilantro (chopped)
1 medium white onion (chopped)
Grated zest of one large lemon
1 cup alfalfa or broccoli sprouts (chopped)
1 cup toasted whole-grain bread crumbs
1 tablespoon extra-virgin olive oil

Directions:
Steam the sprouted garbanzo beans until just tender - about ten minutes.

Combine the garbanzos, egg replacer, and lime salt in a food processor. Puree until the mixture is the consistency of a very thick, slightly chunky hummus. Pour into a mixing bowl and stir in the cilantro, onion, zest, and sprouts. Add the breadcrumbs, stir, and let sit for a couple of minutes so the crumbs can absorb some of the moisture. At this point, you should have a moist mixture that you can easily form into one-inch thick patties. Robert and I like a nice, moist patty because it makes for a nicely textured burger. You can always add more breadcrumbs, a bit at a time, to firm up the dough if need be.

Heat the oil in a heavy skillet over medium low and cook patties for seven to ten minutes, until the bottoms begin to brown. Turn up the heat if there is no browning after ten minutes. Flip the patties and cook the second side for seven minutes, or until golden.

Remove cooked patties from the skillet and cool on a wire rack while you cook the remaining patties.

Serve with a standard setup of lettuce, tomato and onion and don't forget your favorite homemade secret sauce!

89 Ojai Inca Wrap

I was wondering how to fix a healthy burrito that would satisfy my tastes as well as those of my vegan friends. "It would even be better", I told my wife, "if I could make it without flour tortillas so my gluten-free friends could enjoy it too".

I had already decided to use a quinoa filling but needed something to replace the tortilla. My friend, Kris, shared his fresh Ojai-grown collard greens with me a few weeks ago. Seeing them gave me the inspiration for the wrap. Why combine quinoa with collard greens? Two words: Flavor and nutrition. Well, technically that is three words but you get the idea. This wrap is healthy for you. That's the plain and simple of it.

Quinoa was once called the gold of the Incas, who recognized its value in increasing the stamina of their warriors. Not only is quinoa high in protein, but the protein it supplies is complete protein, meaning that it includes all essential amino acids. Collard greens may be the greatest of all commonly eaten cruciferous vegetables, known for their cholesterol-lowering ability. In addition, collards support our detox and anti-inflammatory systems.

If the Incas made wraps, here's how I imagine them doing it in a recipe I call the Ojai Inca Wrap.

Ingredients:
2 small white onions (chopped fine)
1 bell pepper (chopped)
1 tablespoon margarine
2 cups red quinoa (available at Rainbow Bridge)
4 cups water

1 tablespoon Better than Bullion Vegetable Base
½ tablespoon olive oil
1 clove garlic (minced)
28-ounce can crushed tomatoes
1 cup hot vegetable broth
½ teaspoon salt
1 teaspoon sugar
1 tablespoon red chile powder
¼ cup chopped cilantro

Quinoa Directions:
Using a saucepan, sauté half of the chopped onions and all of the bell pepper in margarine until onions are translucent, about five minutes. Add quinoa, water and bullion to sauce pan. Cover and cook for 12 to 14 minutes on medium high. Quinoa should look translucent when fully cooked. Drain excess water from quinoa and set aside.

Sauce Directions:
Heat the olive oil in a frying pan over medium heat. Add the balance of the onions and cook until translucent (about five minutes). Add garlic and cook for another minute or two. Add crushed tomatoes, broth, salt, sugar and chile powder. Stir till well mixed. Simmer uncovered over low heat for approximately 15 to 20 minutes until sauce begins to thicken. Stir in cilantro, remove from heat and set aside.

Assembly Directions:
Lay four collard green leaves out and cut off most of woody stem. Spoon approximately ¾ cup quinoa down the center of each leaf. Layer sauce (approximately two tablespoons each) on top of quinoa. Roll up and trim off ends of leaf (if desired). Serve immediately.

Note: the leaves may be folded into a square to make eating a little easier.

90 Crust-less Quiche

This is a wonderfully quick and easy quiche that can be prepared in less than 20 minutes. It's a great way to introduce your friends to a vegetarian entrée that is tasty, healthy and lower in calories than similar dishes.

If the idea of a crust less quiche is unsettling to you, make it with a crust. I like to save the calories and serve it crust-less with a nice garden salad. Either way you prepare it, it's a delight! If you like hot peppers, seed and slice a couple of jalapeño peppers and sprinkle the slices on top of the quiche before putting it in the oven.

Ingredients:
1 cup sour cream
1 small onion, diced
1 medium zucchini (sliced thin)
1 medium tomato (sliced thin)
1 cup Cheddar cheese (grated)
1 cup Monterey Jack cheese (grated)
10 fresh mushrooms (cleaned and sliced thin)
5 medium eggs
¼ cup milk
½ teaspoon garlic powder
1 teaspoon dried oregano
1 tablespoon butter (melted)

Directions:
Heat oven to 350 degrees.

Spread sour cream on the bottom of a lightly greased pan or baking dish. Sprinkle diced onion over the sour cream, and then layer the zucchini, mushrooms and cheese on top of that. Beat eggs and milk together and pour over veggie layers. Top with slices of tomato. Blend butter, garlic powder and oregano together and pour over top. Bake for 1 hour. Allow to cool for 20 minutes before serving.

91 Tofu Osso Buco

How, you may ask, can one make Osso Buco without meat? After all, doesn't Osso Buco translate to English as "bone with a hole" or "hollowed bone"? With all due respect to my Italian friends, where true Osso Buco is a staple in their household, it's easy to make. Really, it's easy *and* takes approximately half the cooking time of the meat/bone version. This version retains the rich, deep flavors of traditional Osso Buco while substituting organic style tofu cubes for veal.

Ingredients:
1 pound fresh firm organic style tofu
4 tablespoons olive oil
1 sprig fresh rosemary
2 sprigs fresh thyme
2 small bay leaves
3 stalks celery (chopped)
2 carrots (coarsely chopped)
1 medium red onion (coarsely chopped)
½ green bell pepper (chopped)
½ red bell pepper (chopped)
3 cloves garlic (minced)
1 tablespoon balsamic vinegar
2 tablespoons tomato paste
2 cups water
2½ teaspoons Better Than Bouillon vegetable base
¼ cup Marsala wine (white wine works but Marsala works better)
¼ cup brandy
Salt and pepper to taste

Directions:
Cut tofu into 1-inch squares and pat dry with paper towels to absorb excess water. Heat 2 tablespoons of the olive oil over medium heat in a heavy pan. Place tofu in pan and braise, turning on all sides, for about ten minutes. Remove tofu to a plate or dish.

Wrap the rosemary, thyme and bay leaf in cheesecloth and tie with cooking twine. This is a "bouquet garni" that makes it easy to remove herbs that lend flavor but won't cook down. If you've ever made stew and crunched down on a bay leaf that wasn't removed you know what I'm talking about!

Reduce heat on empty pan to medium-low. Add celery, carrot, onion, peppers, garlic and the last two tablespoons olive oil. Sauté for approximately ten minutes. Add bouquet garni, vinegar, tomato paste, water, bouillon, wine and brandy to the pan. Bring to a boil. Add tofu, reduce heat and simmer for approximately 30 minutes.

Remove the bouquet garni. Season to taste with salt and pepper. Serve with your favorite rice dish (Risotto is good) and a tossed green salad for a complete meal. Mangiamo!

Tortellini Pasta Pie

Do you feel like making pasta for dinner but are tired of serving plain old pasta? Dress up your pasta in a little puff pastry.

This is a beautiful dish to serve to friends or family at either an informal or formal dinner setting. How can pasta baked in puff pastry be beautiful? You'll understand what I mean once you slice a wedge and put it on the plate. And because it uses pre-packaged pastry and tortellini, it is quick and easy to make.

Ingredients:
1 package frozen puff pastry sheets (17 1/4 ounces)
2 packages frozen cheese tortellini (12 ounces each)
4 quarts water
2 cups half and half
1 cup fresh grated Parmesan cheese
1/2 cup parsley (chopped)

Directions:
Preheat oven to 425 degrees. Thaw pastry as package directs.

Cook tortellini, uncovered, in four quarts boiling water until al dente (still a bit firm). Drain well in a colander and rinse with cold water to stop the cooking process. In a large bowl, combine tortellini, half and half and cheese.

Roll each sheet of puff pastry out to about 1/4 -inch in thickness. Fit one square of pastry into a 9-inch spring form pan (three inches deep). Let excess pastry drip over rim.

Stir parsley into tortellini mixture and pour mixture into pastry-lined pan. With a sharp knife, cut excess pastry off about ¼-inch from the pan rim and set scraps aside. Place second pastry sheet on top of pie. Pinch edges of pastry sheets together; fold down between pan and pie and crimp to seal securely.

Using a cookie cutter, or a sharp knife, cut the scraps into shapes for decorations. I like heart shapes but any shape will do. Be sure to wet the shapes before placing them wet side on top of the pie. With sharp knife, cut 4 to 6 slashes in top of crust.

Bake pie on lowest rack for about 45 minutes. Let pie cool on rack for ten minutes. To serve, remove pan sides and let stand for another ten minutes before bringing it to the table. Serve with fresh garden salad, vinaigrette dressing and fresh steamed vegetables.

93 Chicken-less Pot Pie

I haven't always been a lacto-ovo vegetarian. There were many meat-based frozen food dishes that my mom popped in the oven when I was a kid and one of them was Swanson's frozen chicken pot pie. Dad and my brother, John, liked the beef and mom liked the turkey. I had the chicken.

One night, many years after leaving home and craving comfort food, I looked in all of our cookbooks to find a good vegetarian recipe for chicken-less pot pie. Nothing was found. Necessity being the mother of invention I created the vegan recipe below.

Mom would have enjoyed this recipe but she worked all day in a job that didn't allow her to sit down. The last thing she wanted to do after work was stand in the kitchen making dinner for us. So when she got home from work she would turn the oven to 425, pick Swanson's pies from the freezer, sit down, put her feet up and wait for the oven to *ding*. I say, "good on ya mom".

Ingredients:
2 tablespoons olive oil
1 large onion (chopped fine)
2 teaspoons garlic (minced)
2 tablespoons whole wheat flour
½ teaspoon dried tarragon
3 carrots (scrubbed and cut into 1-inch pieces)
1 can whole new potatoes (drain liquid - cut into ½ inch cubes)
1 Granny Smith apple (cored and cut into ½ inch pieces)
2 cups water

2½ teaspoons Better Than Bouillon Vegetable Base
½ cup fresh or frozen peas
¼ teaspoon dill
1 can (14.5 ounces) diced tomatoes
Salt and pepper to taste
Bisques (see topping below)

Directions:
Preheat oven to 375 degrees.

Heat the oil in a pot over low heat. Add the onion and cook, stirring occasionally, for ten minutes. Add the garlic and cook for a couple of minutes more. Stir in the flour and tarragon cooking for another couple of minutes.

Add the carrots, potatoes, apple, water and bouillon stirring until the bouillon is completely incorporated. Bring to a boil. Reduce heat to a gentle simmer and cook, covered, for about 15 minutes. Add the peas, dill and tomatoes (including liquid). Season to taste with salt and pepper. Cook for another five to seven minutes.

Spoon the hot vegetable mixture into an ovenproof casserole dish. Use the Bisquick recipe for drop biscuits substituting water or vegetable broth for milk (2¼ cups Original Bisquick and 2/3 cups liquid). Drop biscuit mixture on top of vegetable mixture.

Bake uncovered until biscuit topping is golden brown, about 17 or 18 minutes.

94 Tempeh Stir Fry

This is an easy vegan summer dish to prepare and it doesn't heat the kitchen up much at all. Tasty and nutritious. Give it a *fry*!

Ingredients:
8 ounces soy tempeh (cut into 1/2-inch pieces)
½ cup Tamari sauce
2 tablespoons rice vinegar
4 garlic cloves (minced)
1 teaspoon fresh ginger (minced)
½ teaspoon green curry paste
2 tablespoons water
1 teaspoon agave nectar
1 teaspoon cornstarch
1 tablespoon vegetable oil
¼ cup chopped red bell pepper
4 asparagus stalks (cut into 1-inch lengths)
2 tablespoons green onion (thinly sliced)

Directions:
Steam tempeh cubes for ten minutes. Remove from steamer and transfer to medium mixing bowl. Add soy sauce, vinegar, garlic, ginger and curry paste in a medium bowl. Blend ingredients together. Let marinate for an hour at room temperature.

Strain marinade from tempeh into small bowl. Whisk two tablespoons water, honey and cornstarch into marinade. Set aside.

Heat oil in large nonstick skillet over medium-high heat. Add bell pepper and asparagus and sauté four to five minutes. Add tempeh and sauté for another two minutes. Add marinade mixture and sauté until sauce thickens, about three minutes.

Transfer tempeh stir fry to a serving bowl and sprinkle with green onion. Serve over rice or noodles.

95 Cheese and Mushroom Crepes

I'll bet you think crepes originated in France. Being of Scottish and Irish descent, I must tell you that crepes first originated in Brittany, a former Celtic kingdom, which is now a northwest region of France. Today, crepes are considered a national dish in all of France and are very popular here in the "States".

This is a very tasty dish, especially if you like cheese. Be warned: it is not a "heart-smart" dish by any means. The good news is that it is an easy dish to prepare and assemble. If you *really* like cheese, consider using 2 cups of Swiss cheese instead of the 1½ cups the recipe calls for.

Ingredients:

Crepe Batter:
¾ cup milk
¾ cup water
¼ teaspoon salt
2 tablespoons melted butter (substitute margarine?)
3 eggs
1 cup whole wheat flour

Filling:
1½ pounds fresh mushrooms (cleaned and sliced)
½ cup green onions (chopped)
½ cup butter
1¼ tablespoons fresh basil (chopped fine)
1½ packages Washington's Bullion (or similar)
1½ cups water
¼ cup unbleached white flour
½ cup dry white wine
1 cup heavy cream

Salt and pepper to taste
1½ cups Swiss cheese (grated)

Directions:
Preheat oven to 375 degrees.

The Crepes: Combine all batter ingredients in blender and blend until smooth. Refrigerate for at least one hour prior to making crepes. Cook eight to nine 8-inch crepes (they should resemble thin pancakes) and set aside. Wrap them in plastic or put in a baggie to keep them from drying out.

The Filling: Sauté mushrooms and green onions in ¼ cup of the butter. Add basil and cook until mushrooms are limp. Set aside. Mix bullion in the water. Melt the remaining ¼ cup butter in saucepan. Add flour and cook approximately two minutes. Slowly add bullion mixture, wine and cream. Salt and pepper to taste. Cook over medium heat, stirring constantly, until the sauce thickens. Do not allow to boil. When the sauce is ready, pour 1/3 over the mushroom mixture and allow to cool slightly. Reserve remaining sauce.

Assembly: Fill crepes with mushroom mixture and fold, seam down, in a greased, oven-proof serving dish. I like to fold them into squares but folding them into rolls (like enchiladas) works well too. Pour remaining sauce over the completed crepes and top with Swiss cheese.

Bake for approximately 20 minutes or until cheese is bubbly. Serve with croissants and a fresh garden salad with vinaigrette dressing.

96 Spicy Collard Greens with Basmati Rice

This simple lo-cal vegan dish is easy to prepare, nutritious and because it has the right combination of spices, it's *tasty*.

Ingredients:
2½ cups vegetable broth
1 cup brown basmati rice
1 tablespoon vegan margarine (Earth Balance is good)
½ teaspoon Better Than Bouillon Vegetable Base
¼ teaspoon fresh ground pepper
¼ teaspoon red pepper flakes
2 cups fresh collard greens (rinsed, stems trimmed of stems and chopped)

Directions:
In a large pot, bring the vegetable broth to a boil. Add the rice, vegan margarine, vegetable base, pepper and red pepper flakes. Add the collard greens and bring to a slow simmer. Cover and allow to cook until rice is soft, about 45 minutes.

To serve, drain excess liquid (if any), fluff rice with fork, and let sit for three to four minutes before dishing up.

97 Tamale Pie

It is well documented that the Spaniards were served tamales by the Aztecs during their first visits to Mexico. Those tamales were made with meats, beans and peppers and cooked on open fires. The Aztecs (and I dare say my Mexican friends) would cringe at the thought of bastardizing the tamale by eliminating the meat and putting the beans and peppers in a casserole dish to bake in an oven. But to paraphrase the Immortal Bard: this casserole which we call a tamale by any other name would taste as sweet.

Pie Filling Ingredients:
1 tablespoon olive oil
1 medium onion (chopped fine)
1 medium bell pepper (seeded and chopped fine)
2 cloves garlic (minced)
1 15-ounce can diced tomatoes (include liquid)
1 15 ounce can black beans (drained and rinsed)
1 ear corn - kernels cut off the cob (¾ cup thawed frozen corn)
1 teaspoon chili powder
1 teaspoon ground cumin
½ teaspoon sea salt
Pinch of cayenne pepper

Cornbread Ingredients:
½ cup butter
¼ cup white sugar
2 eggs
1 cup buttermilk
½ teaspoon baking soda
1 cup corn meal
1 cup flour
½ teaspoon salt

Directions:
Preheat oven to 375 degrees.

Heat the olive oil in a large frying pan over medium-high heat. Add the onion, bell pepper and garlic. Cook until softened (about six to eight minutes). Remove from the heat and stir in the tomato sauce, pinto beans, corn, chili powder, cumin, salt and cayenne pepper. Set aside.

Melt butter and pour into a mixing bowl. Stir in sugar. Quickly add eggs and beat well until blended. Stir in buttermilk and baking soda. Stir in corn meal, flour and salt. Blend until few if any lumps remain.

Spread ½ of the cornbread mixture over the bottom of a greased 8x8-inch baking dish. Pour the corn/bean mixture over this layer. Spread the balance of the cooked cornmeal over the top. Bake, uncovered, for 30 minutes. Remove from oven, place aluminum foil cover over pie so the top doesn't burn. Return to oven and bake for another 15 minutes.

Let cool for ten minutes and serve with a side of rice and homemade tortillas.

98 Cheese and Tomato Pie

Allergic to eggs but would love to eat quiche? Here's an egg-less quiche for those that are allergic to eggs or for those that want to avoid the extra cholesterol found in traditional quiches. Fun, easy and delicious but it is loaded with calories. To reduce the calories, substitute butter for olive oil but be aware of the increase in cholesterol as a result of the substitution.

You can also reduce the amount of cheese to ¼ cup. Olives are traditionally high in calories and derive a good portion of their calories from fat. You can substitute ¼ cup chopped red onions for the Kalamata olives but I recommend trying this recipe at least once using the olives. They impart a wonderful flavor that complements the cheeses .

Ingredients:
1 frozen pastry crust (pre-bake at 450 degrees for 12 minutes)
3 tablespoons olive oil
1 clove garlic (minced)
1 28-ounce can diced tomatoes
¾ teaspoon Salt
2 tablespoons fresh parsley (chopped)
½ teaspoon dried basil
Black pepper to taste
2 medium sweet yellow onions
2 tablespoons butter
1/3 cup grated Parmesan cheese
8 ounces mozzarella cheese - grated or cut into thin strips
12 Kalamata olives (pitted and sliced)

Directions:

Preheat oven to 375 degrees.

Heat the olive oil in a large pan and sauté the garlic in it for a few minutes. Add the tomatoes and their juice, ½ teaspoon salt (not all of it), the parsley, basil, and pepper to taste. Simmer this sauce, stirring occasionally, until it is reduced by about half. It should be quite thick. Set aside.

Peel, halve, and thickly slice the onions. Sauté in butter until golden. Sprinkle with ¼ teaspoon salt. Set aside.

Now you can assemble the pie. Sprinkle the Parmesan cheese over the bottom of the pre-baked pastry crust. Arrange the onion slices over Parmesan cheese in an even layer. Cover the onions with the tomato sauce. Arrange the mozzarella cheese evenly on top of the tomato sauce. Sprinkle the olive slices over the mozzarella cheese and bake the pie for 35 minutes. Allow to cool for approximately ten minutes before serving.

99 Lasagna Azteca

This is a Tex-Mex dish that Robin and I enjoyed at Café de la Paz in Berkeley in the gourmet ghetto neighborhood. I tried to duplicate the dish from memory when we returned home and what I came up with was more like Mexican lasagna than the "Tamal Azteca" on the menu at Café de la Paz. Try it and let me know what you think of this original recipe I call Lasagna Azteca.

Ingredients:
1 batch Azteca Sauce (see below)
8 old corn tortillas
1 package frozen spinach, un-chopped, thawed and thoroughly drained (squeeze the water out!)
12 ounces good quality Monterey Jack cheese (grated)
16-ounce package frozen corn (thawed)
¼ cup cilantro (chopped)

Directions:
Preheat oven to 350 degrees.

Lightly grease a baking dish (approximately 7 x 11). Spread a thin layer of sauce over the bottom. Cover sauce with two tortillas. Spread ½ of the spinach (be sure it is thoroughly drained!) over the tortillas. Top with ¼ of the cheese and ¾ cup of sauce.

Place two tortillas on top and press down gently. Spread the corn over the top and cover with ¾ cup sauce and ¼ of the cheese. Place two more tortillas on top and press down. Spread the other half of the spinach on top of the tortillas and cover with ½ of the remaining sauce and ½ of the remaining cheese.

Top with the remaining two tortillas and press down. Spread remaining sauce on the tortillas. Sprinkle remaining cheese on top of sauce. Cover tightly with foil and bake in oven for 25 minutes. Uncover and bake another ten minutes. Sprinkle cilantro on top of each serving.

Azteca Sauce:
Ingredients:
1 small white onion (chopped)
½ tablespoon olive oil
1 clove garlic (chopped)
1 28-ounce can crushed tomatoes (do not drain)
1 cup hot water
1 teaspoon Better Than Bouillon Vegetable Base
½ teaspoon salt
1 tablespoon red chile powder
¼ cup cilantro (chopped)

Directions:
Heat the butter in a frying pan over medium heat (do not burn!). Add onion and cook until translucent (about five minutes). Add garlic and cook for another minute or two. Add crushed tomatoes, water, Better Than Bouillon, salt and chile powder. Stir till well mixed.

Simmer uncovered over low heat for approximately 15 to 20 minutes until sauce begins to thicken. Stir in cilantro, remove from heat and let cool. When still warm (but not hot) puree in blender.

100 Garbanzo Tahini Bake

This is an easy and relatively quick vegan casserole with a good blend of flavors and nutrients. One cup of garbanzo beans (chickpeas), for example, provides 25% of your average daily iron needs. The herbs and capers provide a unique combination of flavors. The neat thing about this recipe is that it makes enough to feed a family of four: including hungry youngsters! Just add a fresh garden salad and your family will be well fed, once again.

Ingredients:
6 cups cooked rice
1 medium onion (diced)
1 15-ounce can diced tomatoes (not drained)
1 15-ounce can garbanzo beans (drained)
1 teaspoon capers
1 teaspoon dried oregano
1 teaspoon dried basil
3 tablespoons tahini
Salt and pepper to taste
1 teaspoon olive oil
1-2 tablespoon sesame seeds

Directions:
Preheat oven to 375 degrees.

Combine rice, onion, tomatoes and garbanzo beans in casserole dish. Add capers, herbs, tahini and salt and pepper. Mix well to make sure the tahini is evenly distributed throughout the mixture.

Cover casserole dish and bake at 375 degrees for approximately 45 minutes, or until top is beginning to brown. Remove from oven, drizzle with olive oil and sprinkle liberally with sesame seeds. Turn the oven up 400 degrees and return casserole, uncovered, for another 15 minutes. Serve bubbling hot!

101 Potato Frittata

This is a wonderfully solid and tasty frittata. I had planned to make it for our friends, Chris and Gaye, who stayed with us over the Super Bowl weekend. As it turned out, we all ended up having a wonderful breakfast with seven other close friends at the Ojai Café Emporium. That breakfast was amazingly good. If they had offered this frittata, however, the breakfast would have been outstanding. It's that good. Give it a try and let me know what you think.

Ingredients:
2 medium-large potatoes (scrubbed and cut into 1" dice)
2 tablespoons olive oil
Salt and pepper to taste
10 eggs
1 medium onion (diced)
1 small jalapeño pepper (seeded and diced fine)
1½ cups shredded cheddar cheese
¼ cup fresh chives (finely chopped)
½ cup sour cream
Additional chives for garnish

Directions:
Preheat oven to 400 degrees.

Combine potatoes in a medium bowl with 1 tablespoon of the oil and the salt and pepper. Transfer to a baking sheet and bake until tender – about 30 minutes. Set aside to cool. The potatoes may be made up to a day ahead of time and stored, covered, in the refrigerator to save prep time.

In a large bowl, whisk in eggs and salt to taste. Add onion, jalapeño, chives and 1 cup of the cheese. Set aside.

Heat 1 tablespoon of the olive oil in a large pan over medium heat. Add potatoes to pan and pour in egg mixture. Reduce heat to medium-low. Cover and cook for five minutes. Then, uncover pan and lift edges to allow uncooked eggs to flow underneath. Cover and cook on low until eggs are set – about ten minutes.

Uncover frittata and sprinkle with balance of cheese. Cover and allow to cook for another three to five minutes on low. To serve, cut into wedges and garnish each wedge with sour cream and chives.

102 Linguini with Roasted Beets

While visiting us over the holidays one year, Robert cooked fresh linguini with caramelized beets, fresh tarragon and caraway seeds. The recipe was too good not to share. Let me know how you like it.

Ingredients:
6 medium red beet roots (washed and trimmed)
½ cup extra-virgin olive oil
1½ teaspoons caraway seeds
1 tablespoons sea salt for the pasta water
16 ounces linguini
4 large garlic cloves (minced)
2 tablespoons balsamic vinegar
½ cup reserved pasta cooking water
¼ cup fresh tarragon (coarsely chopped)
Salt and pepper to taste
Tarragon sprigs as garnish
Extra-virgin olive oil for drizzling

Directions:
Preheat oven to 450 degrees.

Place the beets in a medium baking dish. Fill the pan with 1/2" of water. Cover tightly with foil and bake for 50 to 60 minutes, until tender. Remove from pan and set aside to cool to room temperature.

Peel the beets with the back of a knife. Using a mandolin, cut the beets in 1/16" julienne slices. (If you don't have a mandolin, slice the beets crosswise in 1/8" slices and then cut them in julienned strips.) Transfer to a bowl and set aside.

Heat a large, non-stick heavy-bottomed skillet over high heat. Add the oil, caraway seeds and beets. Sauté for ten to twelve minutes until the beets have caramelized. Toss from time to time (the beet slices will lose their moisture, shrink by half and look very dark around the edges). Remove from heat and set skillet aside.

Bring six quarts of water to a boil. When the water is boiling, add the salt and the pasta. Cook pasta until al dente. Drain well.

While the pasta is draining, return skillet to the stove and heat over high heat. When the beets begin to sizzle, add the garlic and vinegar. Sauté for one minute only, until the vinegar has completely evaporated and glazed the beet slices. Add the pasta, reserved pasta cooking water, fresh tarragon, salt and pepper. Turn off the heat and toss until the pasta is well coated with the sauce.

Garnish with tarragon sprig, drizzle with a little olive oil and serve immediately.

103 Grits with Roasted Poblano Peppers

Here's an Ojai twist on a southern favorite: grits. It's what's for breakfast! Even Paula Dean would like these grits.

Ingredients:
3 cups whole milk
¾ teaspoon salt
¼ teaspoon ground pepper
¾ cup stone-ground grits (yellow or white)
2 garden fresh Poblano peppers
1 tablespoon olive oil
½ large red onion (sliced thin)
Salt and freshly ground pepper
¾ cup aged white cheddar cheese (grated)
2 tablespoons prepared horseradish

Directions:
Bring milk, salt, and pepper to a boil in a medium saucepan. Pour in grits and whisk vigorously to blend. Reduce heat to medium-low and continue cooking, stirring frequently until thickened, about 40 to 45 minutes. Add more liquid (water or milk) as needed. The grits should be done and still hot as you finish preparing the peppers and onion mixtures below.

While the grits are cooking, heat broiler on high. Place the peppers directly under the broiler and cook, turning occasionally, until blistered and blackened on all surfaces, about three to five minutes for each exposed surface. Remove from oven and set aside to cool. Once cooled, run the peppers under a stream of cool water and pull off the blackened skin. Remove seeds and stem. Stack the roasted pepper flesh and cut into thin, ¼-inch-wide, 2-inch-long strips; set aside.

In a medium skillet, heat the oil over medium-low heat. Add the onion, salt, and pepper, and cook, stirring occasionally, until softened and lightly browned, about 15 to 20 minutes. Set aside.

Stir the cheese into the cooked grits until melted. Gently fold in the horseradish, roasted pepper, and sautéed onions. Serve immediately.

104 Curried Butternut and Beets

The secret to tasty Indian food is a good combination of spices. Be assured that this recipe includes an excellent combination of spices. You may not have all of the spices called for below but if you don't it is worth the effort to find them. If you live in Ojai, you can find all of them at Rainbow Bridge Market.

For a complete vegan meal, substitute vegetable oil for the ghee and complement the squash and beets with an equal serving of aromatic basmati rice or Lotus Foods Forbidden Rice.

Ingredients:
1 medium butternut squash (cut into 1-inch cubes)
6 medium beets (cut into 1-inch cubes)
¼ teaspoon coconut oil
¼ teaspoon vegetable oil
½ teaspoon ghee
½ teaspoon asafoetida
1 teaspoon panch phoron (Bengali Five Spice)
¼ cup water
2 teaspoons turmeric
1 teaspoon ground coriander seed
1 teaspoon ground cumin seed
1 teaspoon cayenne
1 teaspoon garam masala (curry powder)
Salt to taste
cilantro for garnish

Directions:
Peel and then cut the squash in half. You can leave the peel on for more nutrition. It cooks well. Clean out the seeds and pulp at the bulbous end (I always wanted to

use the word bulbous. Great word. I can now cross it off my list). Cut squash into 1-inch cubes.

Thoroughly scrub the beets and leave the peel on. Remove the tops and the tips and cut each beet into 1-inch cubes (save the beet greens and lightly sauté later on as a nice vegetable side dish).

In a medium sized pot, heat the oils and the ghee on medium-low heat. Add asafoetida and panch phoron. When seeds start popping, add the beets and the squash. Toss to coat. Cook for approximately three minutes.

Add water, cover and cook on medium-low for another 20 minutes or until beets and squash can barely be pierced with fork tines. Add balance of spices and salt to taste. If vegetables stick to the pan, add another ¼ cup of water. Cover and cook for 20 minutes more on medium-low or until the squash/beets can be easily pierced.

Transfer vegetables to a serving bowl, garnish with cilantro and serve while still warm.

105 Savory Vegetable Tart

This recipe was inspired by a roasted vegetable tart I enjoyed at The Farmer and The Cook's Valentine's Day Dinner. It uses the vegetables and herbs in my Root Vegetables Bake recipe and a whole wheat crust taken from one of my go-to cookbooks, Laurel's Kitchen.

This recipe takes a couple of hours or more to get from oven to the table. The crust takes about ten minutes of prep time and should be refrigerated for at least an hour before rolling out. You might want to make the crust the day before to cut down on prep time when you make the tarts. The filling takes about 15 minutes prep time and an hour and a quarter bake time. The dough and filling should be enough to make six 6-inch diameter tarts after baking.

It's easy to make this vegan. Just substitute Earth Balance spread for the butter and leave off the Parmesan cheese. Be forewarned: this is dish is "dry" so be sure to have a good wine or other beverage at hand to "wet your whistle".

Crust Ingredients:
3 cups whole wheat flour
1 cup wheat germ
1½ teaspoon sea salt
1 cup plus 4 tablespoons butter
10 – 12 tablespoons cold water

Filling Ingredients:
½ pound carrots – about 2 large (scrubbed and cut into ¼-inch lengths)
½ pound red potatoes – about 2 medium (cut ½ inch cubes – scrub but no need to peel)

½ pound rutabaga or turnip – about 1 large (peeled and cut into ½ inch cubes)
½ pound fennel bulb – 1 good size (thinly sliced)
2 tablespoons extra-virgin olive oil
2 teaspoons fresh thyme
1 teaspoons salt
½ teaspoon pepper
2 tablespoon parsley (finely chopped)
¼ cup Parmesan cheese (finely grated)

Crust Directions:
Stir together flour, wheat germ and salt. Cut butter into these dry ingredients (a pastry cutter makes this easy). When the dough is the consistency of rolled oats, sprinkle with enough of the water to hold the dough together. Form into a ball, cover and refrigerate for about an hour.

Filling and Baking Directions:
Preheat oven to 400 degrees.

Place prepared root vegetables in a large baking dish (I use a tall Corning Ware 2.8 liter dish). Drizzle with olive oil, thyme, salt and pepper. Toss to coat. Roast vegetables uncovered for 45 minutes.

Roll out dough and cut into 8 inch circles (this will make a tart about 5 to 6 inches in diameter when you are done). Place a cup of roasted vegetables into the center and spread them out evenly to within 1 inch of the end of the crust. Fold the uncovered crust over the vegetables leaving the center of the tart open.

Sprinkle the open center of each tart with one tablespoon of cheese and a couple of pinches of parsley.

Bake tarts for 25 minutes at 400 degrees. Serve while still hot.

Add a fresh garden salad with vinaigrette dressing and you have a complete meal.

106 Eggplant Parmesan

I had considered naming this recipe Melt-in-Your-Mouth Eggplant Parmesan. I shortened the title but I didn't skimp on any of the ingredients. The secret to tender eggplant is to fry it just right. The secret to the tastiness of this recipe is the combination of herbs and pepper flakes. I have not had better except maybe at Boccali's restaurant. Try this recipe and let me know how it compares.

Ingredients:
3 medium eggplants (cut crosswise into ¼-inch-thick rounds)
3 ¼ teaspoons salt
5 pounds plum tomatoes
1½ cups plus 3 tablespoons olive oil
2 large garlic cloves (chopped fine)
20 fresh basil leaves (tear in half)
¾ teaspoon fresh ground black pepper
¼ teaspoon crushed and dried red pepper flakes
1 cup all-purpose flour
5 large eggs
3½ cups Italian breadcrumbs
2/3 cup Parmesan (finely grated)
16 ounces fresh mozzarella (thinly sliced)

Directions:
Preheat oven to 375 degrees.

Toss eggplant with two teaspoons salt in a colander set over a bowl, then let drain – about 30 minutes.

While eggplant drains, cut a small X in bottom of each tomato with a sharp paring knife and blanch them in a 5-quart pot of boiling water for one minute. Make sure the water is boiling before adding tomatoes. Using a slotted spoon, transfer tomatoes to a cutting board and, when cool enough to handle, peel off skin beginning from scored end. Coarsely chop tomatoes, then purée in batches in a blender.

Heat three tablespoons of the oil in a 5-quart heavy pot over moderately high heat until hot but not smoking. Add garlic and sauté, stirring, until golden, about 30 seconds. Add tomato purée, basil, 1 teaspoon salt, ½ teaspoon pepper, and red pepper flakes. Simmer uncovered, stirring occasionally, until slightly thickened – about 25 to 30 minutes. Set aside.

Stir together flour, remaining ¼ teaspoon salt and remaining ¼ teaspoon pepper in a shallow bowl. Lightly beat eggs in a second shallow bowl. In a third shallow bowl, stir together breadcrumbs and 1/3 cup Parmesan. Set aside all three aside.

Working with 1 slice at a time, dredge eggplant in flour, shaking off excess, then dip in egg, letting excess drip off, and dredge in breadcrumbs until evenly coated. Transfer eggplant to sheets of wax paper, arranging slices in a single layer.

Heat remaining 1½ cups oil in a deep skillet over moderately high heat and fry eggplant for three to four minutes per side. Transfer with tongs to paper towels to drain. Set aside.

Spread 1 cup tomato sauce in bottom of a rectangular (13 x 11-inch) baking dish. Arrange one third of eggplant slices in 1 layer over sauce, overlapping slightly. Cover eggplant with one third of remaining sauce and one third of mozzarella. Continue layering with remaining eggplant, sauce, and mozzarella. Sprinkle top with remaining 1/3 cup Parmesan.

Bake, uncovered, until cheese is melted and golden and sauce is bubbling - about 35 to 40 minutes. Serve with a fresh garden salad and fresh-baked French bread slices hot from the oven.

107 Cannellini Bean Casserole

Cannellini beans are a large white variety of kidney bean very popular in Central and Southern Italy. You may recognize them as the classic bean found in minestrone soup.

I use cannellini in this hearty casserole for a couple of reasons. Using dried cannellini beans gives the dish superior texture *plus* the beans get the chance to soak up all the flavors of the garlic and herbs.

Once you read through the recipe one time, you'll see that this is not a difficult dish to make. It is, however, time consuming but your efforts will be rewarded with unmatched freshness and taste. Here's to cooking in my favorite season of the year, autumn!

Ingredients:
1½ pounds dried cannellini beans (Bob's Red Mill is a good brand)
6 sprigs plus 1½ tablespoons fresh thyme (chopped)
3 sprigs plus 3 tablespoons fresh parsley (chopped)
½ medium white onion (unpeeled)
1 large white onion (diced)
3 whole cloves
1 medium fennel bulb (stalks and fronds reserved; bulb quartered and diced)
12 cloves garlic (6 cloves peeled and halved; 6 cloves minced)
3 tablespoons olive oil
2 cups carrots (diced)
1 teaspoon white wine vinegar
1½ cups fresh breadcrumbs

Directions:
Soak beans in large bowl of cold water overnight. Drain.

Put beans in a 6-quart Dutch oven (I use a 5½-quart All-Clad stainless steel Dutch oven) and add enough water to cover by two inches. Tie together six thyme and three parsley sprigs and add to pot. Pierce onion half with cloves and add to pot. Add fennel fronds and stalks to the pot with the six halved garlic cloves. Partially cover, and bring to a boil. Uncover, reduce heat to medium-low, and simmer 35 to 40 minutes, or until beans are just tender. Drain beans, and reserve cooking liquid. Discard herb bundles, onion, and fennel. Wipe out Dutch oven for next step.

Preheat oven to 400 degrees. Heat two of the tablespoons of oil in Dutch oven over medium-high heat. Add carrots and diced fennel bulb and season with salt, if desired. Cover, and cook ten minutes, or until beginning to brown, stirring frequently. Add the large white diced-onion and cook, covered, for six to eight minutes, or until onion is soft and bottom of pan is browning, stirring occasionally. Add the six cloves of minced garlic, and cook one minute more. It should start to really smell good at this point.

Remove pot from heat and stir in vinegar. Use a spatula to scrape up any browned (caramelized!) bits of onion stuck to the bottom. Add beans, chopped thyme, two tablespoons of the chopped parsley, and 1½ to two cups bean cooking liquid. The total liquid in the pot should come to about 1½ to two inches below top of beans; add more if necessary. Stir well to combine.

Combine breadcrumbs and remaining 1 tablespoon chopped parsley in small bowl. Drizzle remaining one tablespoon oil into crumb mixture, and combine to moisten breadcrumbs. Spread breadcrumb mixture over bean mixture. Bake uncovered for 40 to 45 minutes, or until top is browned and juices have bubbled down below surface, leaving brown rim around edge of crust.

Remove from oven and cool for at least 20 minutes to allow beans to finish absorbing juices. Serve warm with lots of fresh homemade rolls or slices of a good store-bought French bread.

108 Noodle-less Lasagna

I told a friend at the grocery store the other day that I had developed a "noodle free lasagna " recipe using eggplant instead of noodles. "Oh", she said, "you mean eggplant parmesan?" This recipe is similar to eggplant parm but looks and tastes like lasagna. It is a good substitute for regular lasagna for those on a gluten-free diet. Easy, nutritious and all without using lasagna noodles. This recipe makes two servings. Give it a try!

Ingredients:
4 ¼-inch-thick eggplant slices (cut lengthwise from a long, fat eggplant)
1 tablespoon extra-virgin olive oil
1 egg (lightly beaten)
2/3 cup ricotta cheese
1 tablespoon fresh basil (chopped)
1 garlic clove (minced)
¼ teaspoon salt
A pinch of ground nutmeg
1 teaspoon butter (you can substitute olive oil)
8 ounces mushrooms (chopped or sliced)
15 ounces crushed tomatoes
½ tablespoon Italian seasoning
Fresh spinach or baby chard leaves
1 cup mozzarella cheese (grated)
2 tablespoons Parmesan cheese (grated)

Directions:
Preheat oven to 425 degrees.

Pat eggplant slices dry. Rub (or brush) both sides with olive oil and place on cookie sheet. Bake in the oven for about ten minutes and turn slices over. Bake for another ten to 12 minutes or until soft.

Combine egg, ricotta cheese, basil, garlic, salt, and nutmeg in a bowl. Stir well and set aside.

Heat butter in pan over medium to medium-high heat. Do not let it burn. Add mushrooms and cook for four to five minutes or until soft. Stir mushrooms into ricotta mixture and set aside.

Add Italian seasoning to crushed tomatoes and set aside.

Now to assemble the lasagna. Spray a 9x5-inch loaf pan with nonstick spray. Pour ¼ of the tomatoes evenly into the bottom of the pan. Top with one slice of eggplant. Layer spinach leaves over eggplant. Spread half of the ricotta-mushroom mixture on top, followed by another ¼ of the tomatoes. Top with another eggplant slice.

Repeat layering with tomatoes, eggplant, spinach, ricotta-mushroom mixture, tomatoes and the last slice of eggplant. Sprinkle mozzarella cheese followed by the Parmesan cheese.

Reduce oven to 375 degrees and bake lasagna for 20 to 25 minutes or until cheese starts to brown. Serve with a garden-fresh salad and a mellow red table wine.

[119 Date and Fig Nut Tart]

Desserts

109 Ojai Orange Pound Cake

I wanted something different than the traditional Graham family potato cake on my birthday so I searched my folder of dessert recipes and found an orange cake that I haven't made for many moons. This recipe, similar to a traditional pound cake, holds up well even after 20 years. The only change I made is the substitution of healthier coconut sugar for the traditional refined sugar.

Ingredients:

Cake:
3 cups cake flour
1 teaspoon baking powder
Pinch of salt
1 cup butter (room temp)
2 cups coconut sugar
½ teaspoon vanilla
2 tablespoons fresh orange zest (from Ojai oranges)
5 eggs
¾ cup milk

Topping:
¼ cup butter
2/3 cup coconut sugar
½ cup fresh orange juice (from Ojai oranges, of course)

Directions:
Preheat oven to 350 degrees.

Sift together the flour, baking powder and salt. Set aside.

Whip butter with sugar, vanilla and orange zest until

mixture is soft. Add eggs one-by-one, beating well after each addition. Add flour mixture alternating with milk (start and end with the flour). Transfer mixture to a greased Bundt pan and bake for 45 minutes in the center of the oven. Check to see if done in the middle. If not, bake for another ten to 15 minutes.

While cake is baking, place butter, sugar and orange juice in a saucepan and bring to a boil for five minutes. Once cake is done, remove it from the oven and pour topping over cake. Separate sides of cake from pan so the syrup gets in. Cool completely and invert onto dish for serving.

Amaranth Pudding

I was discussing various herbs and grains with my locavore friend Carol (AKA The Chard Lady) the other day. She grows many vegetables and herbs in her garden including amaranth. She asked me if I had any recipes that called for amaranth seeds. I replied "I've heard of it but never cooked with it". She said "I enjoy amaranth and need a few new recipes. You should create a new recipe for me".

I gladly accepted the challenge. To cook with amaranth, however, I first needed to appreciate its history. I found that this grain-like seed has endured for many centuries as an important food source. It means "everlasting" in Greek and served as a highly nutritious gluten-free grain for the ancient civilizations of Central and South America.

The Quechua of Peru use fermented amaranth seed to make a local beer, chicha. Ask me how it is made and I'll tell you why I did *not* try it when visiting the Cusco region a few years ago. The Aztecs of Mexico made a mixture of amaranth into idols that were eaten in their sacrifices and religious rituals. Because of this the Spanish conquistadors abolished the plant to eliminate ritual sacrifices. As a result amaranth was lost, as a food source, to the Americas for hundreds of years.

If you have an intolerance or an aversion to wheat, amaranth is a wonderful substitute. Ounce-for-ounce, it has more protein than wheat being an excellent source of lysine (an essential amino acid). In addition, it is an excellent source of calcium, magnesium and iron. If you like quinoa I think you'll like amaranth.

Here's a vegan amaranth pudding I created for Carol:

Ingredients:
1 cup amaranth seeds
2½ cups water
1 cup unfiltered apple juice
1 tablespoon fresh lemon juice
½ cup white raisins (substitute currents if you want)
½ cup almonds (chopped)
1½ teaspoons vanilla
1 pinch of ground cinnamon
grated rind of one lemon

Directions:
Add amaranth to boiling water, bring back to boil, reduce heat, cover and simmer for 16 - 18 minutes.

Blend juice, raisins, almonds, vanilla, cinnamon and lemon rind until smooth. Combine blended ingredients with two cups cooked amaranth in a large pan. Cover pan and bring to a boil. Reduce heat and simmer for ten to 12 minutes.

Pour pudding into individual dessert bowls. Chill and top with a few fresh grapes or strawberries before serving.

111 Cranberry Christmas Cookies

This is not your traditional Holiday sugar cookie recipe. This is a healthier recipe that's still festive *and* nutritious featuring oatmeal and dried cranberries. Substitute vegan egg replacer for the dairy eggs and this is a vegan recipe.

Ingredients:
1 cup vegetable oil (or use butter)
2 cups coconut sugar (or use 1 cup each brown and white)
2 eggs
2 teaspoons vanilla extract
2 cups flour
1 teaspoon baking soda
1 teaspoon cinnamon
3 cups old fashioned oats
½ cup walnuts (chopped)
1 cup dried cranberries

Directions:
Preheat the oven to 350 degrees.

In a medium mixing bowl, combine the oil and sugar. Mix thoroughly. Beat in the eggs and then the vanilla extract. Set aside.

In a separate, larger bowl, combine the flour, baking soda, cinnamon and oats. To this bowl add the walnuts, cranberries and sugar/egg mixture. Mix well. This mixture will be very thick so be sure to scrape down to the bottom of the mixing bowl so that everything gets mixed thoroughly.

To make the cookies, drop two tablespoons of the

mixture on an ungreased cookie sheet. Continue until the sheet is full. Bake for 15 minutes or until the cookies are golden brown.

Shortbread Cookies

The 1982 Time/Life book, Cookies and Crackers, says, "The art of making cookies and crackers is that of turning simple ingredients into wonderful things..." This recipe is as simple as it gets and creates a wonderfully light, melt in your mouth shortbread cookie. It is simple in that it doesn't call for vanilla flavoring, instant espresso powder, chocolate chips, almonds or lemon zest as with some variations. The use of flour *and* corn starch together give the cookie the "melt in your mouth" texture. And one more thing: it is important to use a good-quality butter (I like a sweet, unsalted butter) and not to use margarine.

Ingredients:
1 cup butter, softened
½ cup confectioner's sugar
¼ cup cornstarch
1½ cups all-purpose flour (whole wheat works well but all-purpose is traditional)

Directions:
Preheat the oven to 375 degrees.

Whip butter with an electric mixer until fluffy. Stir in the confectioners' sugar, cornstarch, and flour. Beat on low for one minute, then on high for three to four minutes. Drop cookies by spoonful's, two inches apart, on an ungreased cookie sheet (if you want to use cookie cutters to shape the cookies, wrap dough in plastic wrap and refrigerate for about an hour before rolling out). Bake for 12 to 15 minutes. Watch that the edges don't brown too much. Cool on wire racks. Serve with coffee or tea although they are great just by themselves!

113 Pumpkin Cookies

Have more garden pumpkins than you and/or your neighbors can handle? Here's a fresh pumpkin cookie recipe that will help use (not waste) your excess pumpkins. Make these for yourself, your kids or your neighbor's kids 'because one leftover pumpkin makes a lot of cookies!

Ingredients:
1 cup cooked pumpkin (*see below)
½ cup coconut oil (or butter, or even olive oil)
¾ cup unrefined sugar (substitute coconut sugar?)
Vegan Egg replacer for 2 eggs (Ener-G works well)
2 cups whole wheat flour
2 teaspoons baking powder
¼ teaspoon sea salt
¼ teaspoon baking soda
½ teaspoon ground cinnamon
¼ teaspoon ground cloves
½ cup walnuts (chopped)

Directions:
Preheat oven to 325 degrees.

Mix all of the ingredients together, adjust spices to your taste, and chill in the refrigerator for 1 hour. Drop by the spoonful onto greased cookie sheets and bake for 8 to ten minutes.

* Cooking the pumpkin: Cut in half, scoop out seeds, place cut side down on baking sheet and bake at 350 until soft – about 30 minutes. Using a sharp knife, cut the skin off the cooked pumpkin. Throw out the skin and mash the good stuff. This will make a few cups of pumpkin good stuff.

114 Bread Pudding

The origin of bread pudding is uncertain. Cooks from many countries and cultures, not wanting to waste stale bread, invented many uses for it including pudding. Today's bread pudding shares these humble roots and adds a few twists depending upon the cook. I like to add apples, walnuts and molasses to mine and serve it with a tasty whiskey sauce.

This can be served any time of the day. I especially enjoy it for breakfast.

Bread Pudding Ingredients:
¼ cup unsalted butter
3 Granny Smith apples (peeled and diced)
1½ cups sugar (divided)
2 tablespoons molasses
¼ cup raisins
¼ cup walnuts (chopped)
1 teaspoon vanilla (divided)
½ teaspoon cinnamon
3 large eggs
1 cup milk
2 cups heavy cream
1/8 teaspoon nutmeg
5 cups bread cubes (I cut up day-old French bread)

Bread Pudding Directions:
Preheat oven to 350 degrees. Prepare a casserole dish with cooking spray.

Melt butter in sauce pan. Add apples, ¾ cup sugar, molasses, raisins, walnuts, ½ teaspoon of the vanilla and all of the cinnamon. Stir to incorporate, remove from heat and set aside.

Lightly beat eggs in a bowl. Add milk, cream, the balance of the sugar and the balance of the vanilla. Add nutmeg and set aside.

Place bread cubes in a large mixing bowl. Add apple and custard mixtures. Mix thoroughly. Spoon bread mixture into the dish and bake for 45 – 60 minutes or until pudding appears solid and light brown.

Serve pudding with the following sauce.

Sauce Ingredients:
2 cups heavy cream
½ cup whole milk
½ cup sugar
2 tablespoons cornstarch
¾ cup Jack Daniels whiskey
Pinch of salt

Sauce Directions:
In a 1-quart saucepan set over medium heat, combine the cream, milk, and sugar. Place the cornstarch and ¼ cup of the whiskey in a small mixing bowl and whisk until blended. Pour this into the cream mixture and bring to a boil. Once the sauce begins to boil, reduce the heat to a gentle simmer and cook, stirring occasionally, for five minutes. Remove the sauce from the heat, add a pinch of salt and the remaining ½ cup of whiskey. Stir to combine and ladle over each piece of bread pudding before serving.

115 Rhubarb Crumble

Rhubarb is a funny vegetable. Not funny *ha-ha* but funny as in *a little different*. When grown in the garden, the stalks look like red chard. If you bite into a stalk, however, it has an ascorbic bite that needs taming. It was used, but perhaps not enjoyed, by sailors to tame scurvy. Ben Franklin is rumored to have brought rhubarb seeds back with him on one of his trips to Europe and that's how it found its way to the Americas.

It is also rumored that an ancient Chinese emperor was given a gift of rhubarb for medicinal use. He was told that it would cure his fever but only after warning him that rhubarb, being a most potent drug, must be taken with great moderation. Don't know how much the emperor was given to take, but I know I can eat this entire recipe in one sitting and come away from the table healthy and with a smile on my face.

Rhubarb is still available at the Ojai Certified Farmers' Market and at your local grocery. But hurry if you want to secure fresh rhubarb with which to make this easy crumble.

Ingredients:
3 cups young rhubarb (diced)
1 tablespoon flour
½ cup coconut sugar
1 teaspoon cinnamon
1/8 teaspoon salt
1 tablespoon water
6 tablespoon vegetable oil
6 tablespoons flour
½ cup brown sugar (firmly packed)
½ cup oats (quick cooking is OK)

Directions:
Preheat oven to 350 degrees.

Combine the first six ingredients in a baking dish. I use a round Corning Ware 1.5 litter dish. Combine the oil, flour and brown sugar in a bowl and mix together until creamy. Add the oats to this and mix until crumbly.

Sprinkle the crumbly mixture over the rhubarb and bake, uncovered, for 40 minutes. Serve hot right out of the oven.

116 Irish Loaf Cake

Yet another quick bread, this loaf cake is enjoyed in Ireland. I like to eat the ends of the bread first. It is traditionally held in Ireland that the end of the loaf of bread (we called it the heel when I was young) is the best part of the loaf.

Ingredients:
1 cup currants
1 ¾ cups sifted all-purpose flour
1 teaspoon double-acting baking powder
¼ teaspoon salt
½ teaspoon mace (or substitute half that much nutmeg)
4 ounces unsalted butter (softened)
1 teaspoon vanilla extract
1 cup minus 2 tablespoons granulated sugar
2 large eggs
½ cup milk
Zest of 2 lemons and 1 large orange
¼ teaspoon caraway seeds

Directions:
Preheat the oven to 350 degrees.

Butter a loaf pan and dust it with fine, dry breadcrumbs. Tap the pan over the sink to shake out excess crumbs.

Cover the currants with boiling water and let stand for five minutes. Drain in a strainer and turn out onto several thicknesses of paper towels. Fold the paper over the currants and press to absorb excess water. Set aside.

Sift together the flour, baking powder, salt, and mace and set these dry ingredients aside.

In a large bowl beat the butter until it is soft. Add the vanilla and then the sugar and mix well. Add the eggs one at a time, beating until thoroughly mixed after each addition. Add about one-third of the dry ingredients, scraping the bowl as necessary with a rubber spatula and beating until incorporated. Gradually add the milk and beat until smooth. Then add the remaining dry ingredients and beat only until smooth.

Stir in the lemon and orange zest. Turn the batter into the prepared pan, smooth the top, and then, with a rubber spatula or with the bottom of a spoon, form a slight trench (about ½-inch deep) down the length of the loaf. That will keep it from rising too high in the middle. Sprinkle the caraway seeds all over the top and bake for 1 hour or until done.

Allow the cake to stand in the pan for about ten minutes, then cover it with a rack, turn over the pan and the rack, remove the pan, and gently turn the loaf right side up to cool on the rack.

Wrap this and refrigerate it for about an hour before serving to develop flavors, and for easier cutting. It is best to cut this with a serrated bread knife.

117 Carrot Cake

This is a basic carrot cake that is moist and delicious. Cut into three inch squares, wrap and freeze for bag lunches, snacks, or just to have on hand. It is just as moist and tasty when defrosted and is one of my favorite breakfast foods.

If this is too basic, try adding a can of crushed (and drained) pineapple to the mix. To save calories, you don't have to add the butter cream frosting. But who wants to save calories when it tastes so good.

Cake Ingredients:
1½ cups salad oil
2 cups sugar
4 eggs
2 cups flour
1 teaspoon salt
2 teaspoon cinnamon
2 teaspoon baking soda
2 teaspoon baking powder
4 cups grated carrots
1 cup chopped walnuts
½ cup raisins

Frosting Ingredients:
8 ounces cream cheese (softened)
8 ounces powdered sugar
½ cup butter
1 tablespoon vanilla

Cake Directions:
Preheat oven to 350 degrees.

Mix oil and sugar together in large mixing bowl. Blend in eggs, one at a time, until mixture is smooth and creamy. Mix in flour, salt, cinnamon, baking soda and baking powder. Add grated carrots and mix thoroughly. Add nuts and raisins and again mix thoroughly.

Lightly grease a 9x13-inch baking pan. Fill with mixture. Bake for one hour or until done when tested in center. Allow to cool for 30 minutes before adding frosting.

Frosting Directions:
Blend cream cheese with butter until smooth. While stirring, gradually add powdered sugar. Add vanilla. Beat mixture until creamy smooth. If not creamy enough to spread, a little water may be added, a half-teaspoon at a time, until just right.

118 Spicy Apple Cake

This is a moist, tasty cake that is best shared with friends. I like it best served cold. Robin likes it with a scoop of vanilla ice cream.

Ingredients:
2 cups flour
2 ½ teaspoons cinnamon
2 teaspoons baking powder
1 ½ cups sugar
1 teaspoon salt
2 eggs (beaten)
¾ cup oil
2 teaspoons vanilla
4 cups apples (peeled and diced)
1 cup walnuts (chopped)

Directions:
Preheat oven to 350 degrees.

Mix first five ingredients together and set aside. In a separate bowl, mix remaining five ingredients and set aside. Now mix both batches of ingredients in a large mixing bowl. The mixture should be very thick so don't worry. Prepare a Bundt pan and spoon mixture into pan. Bake for 55 to 60 minutes or until done.

Remove cake from oven and let cake cool for 15 minutes. Invert cake onto serving dish and when completely cool, apply a light dusting of powdered sugar.

119 Date and Fig Nut Tart

If you've got a sweet tooth, this recipe is a way to fulfill your craving for something sweet. It features dates, which are naturally sweet, low in sodium, rich in potassium and contain a fair amount of selenium (selenium can help lower the risk of heart disease as well as help keep our immune system healthy).

Now, even though dates are very nutritional by themselves, I'm not saying this is a super-nutritional recipe. Far from it. In addition to the dates, it includes a lot of other sweet tasting carbohydrates such as figs, cranberries, brown sugar and honey. So if you need to watch your sugar intake, this may not be the best recipe for you. I will say that it is a good recipe and that your friends and family, who need that once-in-a-while sugar infusion, will enjoy eating it.

Ingredients
1 large egg
2½ tablespoons golden brown sugar (firmly packed)
2½ tablespoons butter (melted)
2 tablespoons orange blossom honey
1¾ teaspoons orange peel (finely grated)
½ cup unsalted pistachios (shelled)
3¼ cups pitted Medjool dates (halved lengthwise)
½ cup dried cranberries
½ cup dried black Mission figs (stemmed and halved)
Tart crust (see below*)
1 cup Greek yogurt

Directions:
Preheat oven to 350 degrees.

Line baking sheet with parchment paper. Whisk egg,

two tablespoons brown sugar, two tablespoons melted butter, honey, and one teaspoon orange peel in medium bowl.

Set aside one tablespoon of the nuts for garnish. Add remaining nuts and all dried fruit to bowl with egg mixture; toss filling to coat.

Unroll crust onto prepared sheet. Spoon filling into center of crust; spread out in even layer, leaving 1½ to 2-inch border. Fold crust edges over filling (about an inch of the outside crust) pleating occasionally. Brush crust with remaining ½ tablespoon melted butter. Finely chop reserved tablespoon of nuts. Mix chopped nuts and remaining ½ tablespoon brown sugar in small bowl. Sprinkle over crust.

Bake tart until crust is golden brown and filling is bubbling in center, about 40 minutes. Stir yogurt and remaining ¾ teaspoon orange peel in small bowl. Serve tart warm or at room temperature with orange-flavored yogurt on the side.

* Crust
Ingredients:
3 cups flour
1 cup wheat germ
1½ teaspoon sea salt
1 cup plus 4 tablespoons butter
10 – 12 tablespoons cold water

Directions:
Stir together flour, wheat germ and salt. Cut butter into these dry ingredients (a pastry cutter makes this easy). When the dough is the consistency of rolled oats, sprinkle with enough of the water to hold the dough

together. Form into a ball, cover and refrigerate for about an hour before rolling out into a circle approximately ¼-inch thick.

120 Vegan Bundt Cake

This is a solid vegan cake with a wonderfully fresh lemon flavor.

Ingredients:
1 tablespoon Earth Balance Spread (melted)
2 tablespoons flour
3½ cups flour
1 tablespoon Nutiva organic shelled hempseed
1 ½ teaspoon aluminum-free baking powder
¾ teaspoon baking soda
¾ teaspoon salt
1 cup unsweetened plain soymilk
1 tablespoon lemon zest
½ cup lemon juice
1¼ cups light agave nectar
½ cup canola oil

Directions:
Preheat oven to 350 degrees. Grease and flour Bundt pan using Earth Balance vegan spread and 2 tablespoons flour.

In a large bowl, mix 3½ cups flour, hempseed, baking powder, baking soda and salt; whisk to combine. Set aside.

In a separate bowl, mix soymilk, lemon zest and lemon juice; let stand five minutes. Whisk in agave nectar and oil.

Stir soymilk mixture into flour mixture. Pour batter into prepared pan, and bake for one hour, or until toothpick inserted in center of cake comes out clean. Cool in pan, then unmold. If you like your cake with icing, be sure the cake cools before applying icing. Me? I like it just fine without icing.

121 Egg and Gruyère Strata

So what is a strata? Wikipedia says that it is "a family of layered casserole dishes in American cuisine." I say it is a great way to use leftover or stale bread. Here's my take on traditional strata. Serve it for breakfast or brunch. Either way it is sure to satisfy.

Ingredients:
6 thick slices multi-grain bread (leftover or stale is best)
2 large eggs
1 cup milk (slim is good but whole is better)
2 teaspoons stone ground mustard
6 ounces Gruyère cheese (grated)
Salt and ground black pepper to taste
4 asparagus spears (remove woody part of stems)
1 tablespoon fresh chives (chopped)

Directions:
Preheat the oven to 350 degrees. Spray a 9x9-inch baking dish with cooking spray.

Remove the crusts from the bread and cut into cubes. Slice the remaining bread into 2-inch strips. Lay the bread strips across the baking dish, slightly overlapping. If they come up the sides of the dish that's OK. Add bread cubes to the bottom of the dish (over slices).

Whisk the eggs, milk and mustard in a large bowl. Stir in half of the cheese and season with salt and pepper. Pour three-fourths of this mixture over the bread cubes. Place asparagus spears on top then pour the remaining egg mixture over the top and finish with the remaining cheese. Cover and refrigerate for 30 minutes (or more) before baking.

Bake the strata until just set, 30 to 35 minutes. Let cool ten minutes, sprinkle the top with chopped chives, and serve while still warm.

Note: Once the strata is complete, you can cover it (unbaked) and refrigerate overnight until you are ready to bake the next morning. This recipe serves two and can easily be doubled to serve four.

How I Became A Vegetarian

I gave up all meat and fish one day in August 1975.

I had just started graduate school at San Diego State University and worked half time on campus in a small library. My co-workers were vegetarians.

One day they asked me if I knew anything about vegetarianism. I told them that I had taken a nutrition class as an undergraduate at U.C. Berkeley in 1972 and that a few of the lectures focused on vegetarian diets, how to combine foods for "complete" protein, where to find foods with essential fatty acids, and the importance of taking vitamin B-12 supplements if you didn't eat meat or fish.

I took this class because my roommate, Lol, and I didn't really have a lot of extra cash for food. There was little if no meat in our refrigerator. Ever. We got our beef fix if we went home for the weekend or visited with friends and stayed long enough to be invited to sit with them for dinner.

If I was forced into a diet with little or no meat, I wanted to know what I was doing to my body. That class taught me well. The vegetarian basics and the benefits of a vegetarian lifestyle that I learned at U.C. Berkeley in 1972 served me well in 1975 as I contemplated a vegetarian diet.

After working in San Diego with my new vegetarian friends for just one week, I made a commitment to eliminate meat and fish from my diet and to eat as healthy as possible. With these new friends as my support group, I made the transition, but it wasn't always easy.

Life as a fledgling lacto-ovo vegetarian during the mid '70s was interesting. My brother had just moved to Texas, and they taunted him mercilessly about his "California flake of a brother." But that's another story for another time.

In the fall of 1976, I was working as a graduate student assistant for the California State Department of Education. I was living in San Diego, headquartered in Sacramento, and working 5 days a week in the Los Angeles basin, where I rented a room by the week, out of a low-cost motel at 3rd and Vermont. By low-cost, I mean sleazy. By being thrifty on lodging, however, my per diem went a lot further toward a good vegetarian meal than it would have otherwise.

Money or not, I had a hard time getting a good meal without worrying about the meal being truly vegetarian. This is not to say there weren't good vegetarian restaurants, but the good ones were few and far between.

While working in Los Angeles, I remember asking for a "vegetarian" pizza at a pizza restaurant on Pico Boulevard. The closest thing on the menu was a plain cheese pizza, and it was politely pointed out to me that was all they offered to vegetarians. The manager heard me at the counter and asked if he could be of help. He seemed eager to help, so I explained what I meant by vegetarian, and he said, "no problem."

I paid for the pizza and a beer and took a seat at a table near the salad bar. To my amazement, the manager brought out my pizza, loaded it with stuff from the salad bar, and proudly served it to me 20 minutes later. Iceberg lettuce baked for 20 minutes in a 400-degree oven does not a vegetarian pizza make. At least the beer was cold and refreshing.

One vegetarian restaurant that never disappointed was in Venice. It had an excellent name: The Marathon Meatless Messhall. It had excellent food, as well, and was funky and fun. It was right on the beach and was a hangout for a lot of interesting folks. Bob Dylan, for example, was a regular.

Another popular vegetarian restaurant, The Prophet, was located on University Avenue in San Diego. When you walked in, you were escorted to a table that was at just the right height for eating. The right height that is, if you sat on the floor with legs folded in the lotus position. Lucky for me, I found this comfortable. I loved eating there when I could afford it. They served a side dish of brown rice steamed with garlic, tarragon, and basil leaves. A friend worked there and gave me the recipe. I still make this rice and never tire of it.

The good news today is that most restaurants will accommodate a lacto-ovo vegetarian even if there are no vegetarian items on their menu. The even better news is that there is now a plethora of excellent vegetarian restaurants throughout California. Two are right here in Ojai. My appetite and I will be forever in debt to The Farmer and The Cook and HIP Vegan Cafe.

The Valley Vegetarian Website
[valley-vegetarian.com]

At my Valley Vegetarian website, you'll find my thoughts on a vegetarian lifestyle, vegetarian recipes, and information on local restaurants, markets, and farms that support a vegetarian lifestyle.

How do I define vegetarianism? There are lacto-ovo vegetarians who eat eggs and dairy products and lacto vegetarians who eat dairy products but no eggs. There are semi and demi vegetarians that eat less meat than the average person and may eat fish.

There are vegans whose diet does not include animal products at all, and there are fruitarians who only eat foods that don't kill the plant and consume mainly raw fruit, nuts, and grains. A pescatarian is a vegetarian who also consumes fish.

Which one am I? I am a lacto-ovo vegetarian. My recipes are mainly lacto-ovo, but many are vegan and gluten-free. Nothing fancy just good, home-style cooking. Many of my recipes have been previously published in the Ojai Valley News and the Carpinteria Coastal View News.

My hope is that all vegetarian lifestyles will benefit, if only a little, from my efforts. Let me know what you think. I look forward to hearing from you!

Index of All Recipe Titles (Alpha)

Amaranth Pudding (110)
Arugula Walnut Pesto Salad (22)
Baked Potato Soup (29)
Banana Nut Bread (7)
Bannock Bread (1)
Basil Pesto (70)
Boiling Onions and Raisins (39)
Bread Pudding (114)
Broccoli-Ricotta Cheese Pie (87)
Cabbage Soup (34)
California Dreamin' Burger (83)
Cannellini Bean Casserole (107)
Caprese Salad (23)
Carrot Cake (117)
Cheese and Mushroom Crepes (95)
Cheese and Tomato Pie (98)
Chevre Chaud Salad (13)
Chicken-less Pot Pie (93)
Chicken-less Salad (20)
Chives Vegetable Dip (75)
Chow Chow (51)
Citrusy Kumquat Chutney (65)
Cranberry Christmas Cookies (111)
Crust-less Quiche (90)
Curried Butternut and Beets (104)
Date and Fig Nut Tart (119)
Dog Biscuits (64)
Edamame Salad (12)
Egg and Gruyere Strata (121)
Eggplant and Bell Pepper Terrine (24)
Eggplant Parmesan (106)
Epazote Black Beans (78)
Esquites (37)
Fenugreek Potatoes (45)

Flatbread (10)
Fresh Carrot Salad (19)
Fresh Fruit Risotto (42)
Garbanzo Tahini Bake (100)
Gluten-Free Tabouli (25)
Gran's Carrot Casserole (35)
Grits with Roasted Poblano Peppers (103)
Guacamole (67)
Guinness Potato Salad (21)
Hachiya Smoothie (53)
Idaho Potatoes (36)
Irish Fondue (85)
Irish Loaf Cake (116)
Irish Soda Bread (3)
Italian Bread Salad (16)
Jalapeño Cheese Bread (6)
Jalapeño Corn Chowder (28)
Jalapeños in Escabeche (52)
Japanese Eggplant (43)
Knishes (56)
Lasagna Azteca (99)
Leek and Potato Soup (31)
Lemongrass Tofu (82)
Lentil Soup (32)
Linguini with Roasted Beets (102)
Lo-Cal Potato Salad (62)
Magic Oatmeal (48)
Matzo Ball Soup (27)
Mexican Hominy Bake (86)
Middle Eastern Dip (54)
Mint Iced Tea (77)
Mom's Popovers (4)
Mulligatawny Soup (30)
Mushroom and Garlic Tapas (68)
Noodle-less Lasagna (108)
Nopale Salsa (46)

Nutty Meatloaf (80)
Oatcakes (8)
Ojai Inca Wrap (89)
Ojai Mojo (63)
Ojai Orange Pound Cake (109)
Oregano Chilaquiles (72)
Parsley Brown Rice (76)
Persimmon and Spinach Salad (11)
Peruvian Cornbread (5)
Pico de Gallo (50)
Pimiento Cheese Spread (58)
Plantains with Chipotle Dip (40)
Potato Frittata (101)
Potatoes Au Gratin (41)
Pumpkin Cookies (113)
Quinoa Salad (17)
Raw Beet Salad (18)
Rhubarb Crumble (115)
Rice Cakes with Habanero Sauce (61)
Roasted Red Pepper Sauce (57)
Root Vegetables Bake (44)
Rosemary Pasta Sauce (74)
Rosti (38)
Salsa Verde (47)
Robin's Tortilla Soup (33)
Savory Vegetable Tart (105)
Scots Scones (9)
Shallot Vinaigrette (60)
Shortbread Cookies (112)
Simple Lettuce Wraps (66)
Spicy Apple Cake (118)
Spicy Collard Greens with Basmati Rice (96)
Spicy Fava Bean Salad (15)
Spoon Bread (2)
Sprouted Burger (88)
Sundried Tomatoes and Eggplant Spread (69)

Tamale Pie (97)
Tarragon Creamy Dressing (71)
Tempeh Stir Fry (94)
Tofu Osso Buco (91)
Thyme Cream Cheese Spread (73)
Tofu Frittata (84)
Tortellini Pasta Pie (92)
Two-Tone Coleslaw (26)
Valley Vegetarian Burger (79)
Vegan Bundt Cake (120)
Vegetarian Gravy (59)
Vegetarian Meatballs (81)
Vodka Sauce (49)
Welsh Rarebit (55)
Wheat Berry Salad (14)

Index of Vegan Recipes (Alpha)

Amaranth Pudding (110)
Arugula Walnut Pesto Salad (22)
Basil Pesto (70)
Boiling Onions and Raisins (39)
Cabbage Soup (34)
Cannellini Bean Casserole (107)
Caprese Salad (23)
Chicken-less Pot Pie (93)
Chicken-less Salad (20)
Chow Chow (51)
Citrusy Kumquat Chutney (65)
Dog Biscuits (64)
Edamame Salad (12)
Eggplant and Bell Pepper Terrine (24)
Epazote Black Beans (78)
Fenugreek Potatoes (45)
Flatbread (10)
Garbanzo Tahini Bake (100)
Gluten-Free Tabouli (25)
Guacamole (67)
Jalapeños in Escabeche (52)
Japanese Eggplant (43)
Knishes (56)
Lemongrass Tofu (82)
Lentil Soup (32)
Linguini with Roasted Beets (102)
Magic Oatmeal (48)
Middle Eastern Dip (54)
Mulligatawny Soup (30)
Mushroom and Garlic Tapas (68)
Nopale Salsa (46)
Ojai Inca Wrap (89)
Ojai Mojo (63)
Parsley Brown Rice (76)

Persimmon and Spinach Salad (11)
Pico de Gallo (50)
Potatoes Au Gratin (41)
Quinoa Salad (17)
Raw Beet Salad (18)
Rhubarb Crumble (115)
Rice Cakes with Habanero Sauce (61)
Salsa Verde (47)
Simple Lettuce Wraps (66)
Spicy Collard Greens with Basmati Rice (96)
Spicy Fava Bean Salad (15)
Sprouted Burger (88)
Sundried Tomatoes and Eggplant Spread (69)
Tarragon Creamy Dressing (71)
Tempeh Stir Fry (94)
Tofu Osso Buco (91)
Tofu Frittata (84)
Two-Tone Coleslaw (26)
Vegan Bundt Cake (120)
Vegetarian Gravy (59)
Wheat Berry Salad (14)

Index of Gluten-Free Recipes (Alpha)

Amaranth Pudding (110)
Basil Pesto (70)
Boiling Onions and Raisins (39)
Cabbage Soup (34)
Chicken-less Salad (20)
Chives Vegetable Dip (75)
Chow Chow (51)
Citrusy Kumquat Chutney (65)
Crust-less Quiche (90)
Curried Butternut and Beets (104)
Edamame Salad (12)
Eggplant and Bell Pepper Terrine (24)
Epazote Black Beans (78)
Esquites (37)
Fenugreek Potatoes (45)
Fresh Carrot Salad (19)
Fresh Fruit Risotto (42)
Garbanzo Tahini Bake (100)
Gluten-Free Tabouli (25)
Guacamole (67)
Hachiya Smoothie (53)
Jalapeño Corn Chowder (28)
Jalapeños in Escabeche (52)
Japanese Eggplant (43)
Lemongrass Tofu (82)
Lentil Soup (32)
Mexican Hominy Bake (86)
Mint Iced Tea (77)
Mulligatawny Soup (30)
Noodle-less Lasagna (108)
Nopale Salsa (46)
Nutty Meatloaf (80)
Ojai Inca Wrap (89)
Ojai Mojo (63)

Parsley Brown Rice (76)
Persimmon and Spinach Salad (11)
Pico de Gallo (50)
Pimiento Cheese Spread (58)
Plantains with Chipotle Dip (40)
Potato Frittata (101)
Quinoa Salad (17)
Rice Cakes with Habanero Sauce (61)
Roasted Red Pepper Sauce (57)
Robin's Tortilla Soup (33)
Root Vegetables Bake (44)
Rosemary Pasta Sauce (74)
Salsa Verde (47)
Shallot Vinaigrette (60)
Spicy Collard Greens with Basmati Rice (96)
Spicy Fava Bean Salad (15)
Sundried Tomatoes and Eggplant Spread (69)
Tofu Osso Buco (91)
Thyme Cream Cheese Spread (73)
Tofu Frittata (84)
Two-Tone Coleslaw (26)
Vodka Sauce (49)

Please turn the page for a
preview of the

*Ojai Valley Vegetarian Blog:
A Companion to the Ojai Valley
Vegetarian Cookbook*

Now available at Amazon.com

8. Aromas and Memories

Helen Keller once said, "Smell is a potent wizard that transports us across thousands of miles and all the years we have lived."

When I smell freshly baked bread, I remember the pastries at Shubert's Bakery on Clement Street in San Francisco. I worked with my dad in the Geary Ford parts Department at 12th and Geary. I couldn't afford the pastries very often, but I would walk the few short blocks to the shop every day, at lunchtime, to experience their fresh-baked aroma. The buttery Danish filled with cream cheese was my favorite. I can still see it in my mind's eye. Mouthwatering.

A whiff of chard greens takes me back in time to the late 50s and family dinners at Banchero's restaurant in Hayward. Biting into a fresh peach reminds me of picking peaches at Gran's house in prep for two days of canning. Walking into a friend's home and smelling a roast in the oven reminds me of my mom's Sunday pot roast complete with carrots, potatoes, and onions.
The varied aromas at Thanksgiving remind me of Nana's house in the Central Valley. I couldn't wait to jump out of the car and run up the steps to the porch. As soon as I opened the front door, my senses were overwhelmed with the aroma of turkey in the oven and pumpkin pies cooling on racks in the kitchen. I could hardly wait to eat.

I recently asked my friends the following question, What is your favorite cooking aroma, and what memories does it invoke? Here are their responses:

Strawberries and figs cooking over the stove to make strawberry fig jam. My mom used the hard wax to seal the jar. Yummmm. – Elana D.

The smell of bread and cinnamon rolls baking=my Mom. – Sharon G.

Nothing smells as good as a tree-ripened Ojai orange or Pixie! – Suza F.

Oh, so many. Shall I start with my grandmother's cooking Mexican food, my mom's cooking, how can I recount the many memories? I do recall one of my favorite smells was and still remains, sitting in the Santa Barbara harbor with the view of the bobbing boats and the smell of freshly cooked seafood at Brophy's Restaurant under a cool marine layer. - Brenda M.

Gingerbread ~~ takes me way back. – Barbara G.

GARLIC all the way... – Moses K.

I have none? However, I sure do hope I created some! – Robin B.

I love the smell of lots of things now, but few of them are as emotionally loaded as smells of things cooking in my mother's kitchen. – Crystal D.

Coffee for me, and cinnamon sticks in winter. I could go on and on, waxing poetic...- Theresa S.

My mother is Vietnamese so the smell of lemon, mint, chili paste, cilantro, and fish sauce would be my most favorite aromas coming out of the kitchen. – Michelle M.

Dungeness Crab...getting out of the car at the wharf in San Francisco and that smell of the Dungeness crab pots smacking my sniffer, then taking the crab home and the smell of it boiling on the stove and then cracking it on the table covered in newspapers. - John G.

For me, it was Aunt Elaine and Mom's roast with gravy that only they could make with such a savoy taste. – Sandy W.

Tortillas cooking and coffee brewing were my childhood morning scents. – Beth E.

Two of my favorite aromas are bacon and sautéed onions with garlic, but food does not remind me of a specific time or place. My real aroma memories are of pre microwave, air conditioning, prepared food, and fast food days when women cooked dinner from scratch with open kitchen windows. Riding bicycles or skating through the neighborhood, one could tell what was being served by the wonderful smells in the air. – MJ

Nutmeg...- Pam P.

The smell of percolating coffee, sugar and cinnamon. That takes me back to my Grandma's kitchen when she used to let me use the pie crust dough to make my own little pie crust treats after she made her lemon cream pie. – Donna L.

The aroma of eastern Indian curries. While I do not eat curries or enjoy their particular flavor at this time in my life, it does strongly remind me that I was living in India in a not-so-distant previous life! – Nancy S.

My mother was a bit of a gourmet cook. I remember the stringent aroma of tarragon and vinegar simmering in a double boiler to make béarnaise sauce on our kitchen stove. The aroma would fill the house, wafting up to the second story. Mom would keep a small butter tub of the béarnaise in the fridge and pull it out every time we grilled filets on the barbeque by the pool. Looking back now, I realize from where my blessing (or is it a curse?) of fine taste came. I was a bit dismayed to find that not all fridges came so well stocked when I left home. – Gay M.

Hayward in the 50s also. Cookies baking in the oven when I came home from school was the best. – Judith B.

The smell of pinto beans cooked with a couple of ham hocks accompanied by the smell of cornbread cooking in the oven. I have such great memories of sitting at the table, devouring these beans, and the thick tasty stock they were in. We would all save half of the cornbread and crumble into our milk glasses with a little sugar for dessert. – Jodi B.

At Christmas, my mom used to make these wonderfully crisp and tender Norwegian pastries called rosettes. She had a flower-shaped iron that she dipped into a batter and then fried them in very hot oil. When they were golden in color, she would take them out of the oil and sprinkle them with powder sugar. She always let us kids eat them as soon as they were cool enough to handle. They tasted so sweet and good and full of love. – Robin G.

The yummy smell of apple pie baking and fond memories of my Grandmother Lahey's kitchen assembling and cooking at least ten apple pies...2 for each family...Red, Jimmy, Danny, Graham, and my mom's family...all good. I also think of my mom every time I smell mushrooms sautéed in red wine, butter, and fresh herbs...they were the best and one of my favorites to still make. Oh...how could I forget my sister Karen's blue cheese biscuits...Karol B.

Okra being cooked along with tomatoes and corn in a frying pan. – Elaine N.

The smell of fresh-cut veggies on my lover's hands used to be the most erotic thing in my young life. O...did I write that out LOUD...;-o – Theresa S.

My mother's garden. It was small, but she worked really hard in it, and it was lush and green and fed our family of five very well. We did not have much money. But having that garden was the reason we never experienced the feeling of going hungry. The smell of fresh-cut rosemary invokes a feeling of comfort and relief. - like the world is a good place after all. – Claudia W.

I love the smell of yeast- I always take a little 'smell' when I initially open the jar and I love the wonderful, wafting trail throughout my home as I bake bread - My memories are fond due to my sweet grandmother Alfreda - she was always making bread - She had a funny metal bucket looking contraption that connected to the counter with a "C" clamp, it was her "bread machine". She'd toss all her ingredients into the bucket, put the lid on and then she'd crank it to "knead" the dough - My brother and I were often enlisted to crank as well - Once it had risen, she'd pop it into the oven. My brother and I would get distracted doing something else until the amazing aroma gently wafted throughout - We'd sneak a peek to see if it was ready - We were all too eager to get a fresh, warm slice of Grandma's bread! – Suze M.

Thank you, my friends, for sharing your aromas and memories. - Rand

Made in the USA
Las Vegas, NV
14 April 2021